Fundamentals of C++

ACTIVITIES WORKBOOK *Introductory Course*™

Dr. Kenneth A. Lambert
Washington & Lee University

Dr. Douglas W. Nance
Central Michigan University

COURSE TECHNOLOGY™

THOMSON LEARNING

Australia • Canada • Mexico • Singapore • Spain • United Kingdom • United States

COURSE TECHNOLOGY
THOMSON LEARNING

Fundamentals of C++ , Introductory Course
by Dr. Kenneth A. Lambert and Dr. Douglas W. Nance

Managing Editor:
Melissa Ramondetta

Senior Product Manager:
Dave Lafferty

Production Editor:
Christine Spillett

Printer:
Mazer

Fee Writer and Consulting Editor:
Custom Editorial Productions, Inc.,
Tom Bockerstette

Marketing Manager:
Kim Wood

Cover Design:
Abby Scholz

Compositor:
GEX Publishing Services

Contents

LESSON 1   COMPUTER SCIENCE, COMPUTER ARCHITECTURE, AND COMPUTER LANGUAGES

FILL IN THE BLANK

Complete the following sentences by writing the word or words in the blanks provided.

1. A(n) _____ is a set of instructions that will eventually lead to the solution of a problem.

2. _____ is information in the form of characters that is manipulated by a machine.

3. In order for more than one computer user to share resources (i.e. printers, etc.) a _____ is necessary.

4. A set of instructions that tells the computer what to do is called a(n) _____.

5. The type of computer we are currently working on is a(n) _____.

6. Programs such as word processors, games, and operating systems are called _____.

7. Computers store information in the form of _____ in their memory.

8. A keyboard would be considered a(n) _____ device.

9. A printer would be considered a(n) _____ device.

10. A necessary program that allows the user to communicate with the machine is a(n) _____.

11. An example of a low-level language is _____.

12. C++, Pascal, COBOL, Logo, and BASIC are all examples of _____.

13. _____ must be run through a compiler to create an object code file.

14. A(n) _____ is a combination of 8 bits used to represent a single character.

15. _____ is a set of numeric values used to represent letters, symbols, and numeric values in a computer.

16. A(n) _____ is a program that translates source code or byte codes into machine language while the program is being executed.

17. A major hardware component that consists of the arithmetic/logic unit and the control unit is the _____.

TRUE/FALSE

Circle T if the statement is true or circle F if the statement is false.

T   F   1. A logical sequence of instructions that tells a computer how to perform a specific task is an instruction set.

T   F   2. Program instructions must be converted into machine language before a microprocessor can execute them.

T   F   3. COBOL is an example of a low-level programming language.

T   F   4. Compiled programs require more memory than interpreted programs.

T F **5.** The most important thing that a computer science student can do is learn keyboarding efficiently.

T F **6.** A program is a set of instructions that tells the machine what to do.

MULTIPLE CHOICE

Select the best response for the following statements.

1. A program that can be used to create source code and save the files in a text format is called a(n)
   a. code generator.
   b. compiler.
   c. interpreter.
   d. text editor.

2. Which of the following is **not** an example of a high-level language?
   a. BASIC
   b. COBOL
   c. Assembly
   d. C++
   e. All of the above.

3. The physical machine and devices that support it is called
   a. software.
   b. CPU.
   c. physical support.
   d. hardware.
   e. None of the above.

4. The following is **not** an example of an output device
   a. keyboard.
   b. printer.
   c. monitor.
   d. speaker.
   e. Both a and d.

5. Which of the following is considered your computer's primary storage?
   a. Read-only memory (ROM)
   b. Floppy disk
   c. Hard disk
   d. Random access memory (RAM)
   e. Both a and d.

6. Which of the following is an advantage of a high-level programming language?
   a. It normally contains fewer programming errors than a low-level language.
   b. It is easier to move among computers with different microprocessors than a low-level language.
   c. It is more easily read than a low-level language.
   d. All of the above.

7. A set of steps that a computer can follow to achieve a desired result is a(n)
   a. object file.
   b. process.
   c. instruction set.
   d. algorithm.
   e. None of the above.

8. Compilers are programs that read source code files and convert them into
   a. text files.
   b. readable code.
   c. assembly code.
   d. machine code.
   e. None of the above.

MATCHING

Place the letter of the keystroke on the right that will execute the highlight movement on the left.

_____ 1. Characters that are used to represent information.   a. algorithm

_____ 2. Physical support devices for the machine.   b. data

_____ 3. A large computer typically used by universities.   c. hardware

_____ 4. Programs designed for a specific use.   d. software

_____ 5. A sequence of statements written to solve a problem.   e. mainframe

WRITTEN QUESTIONS

Write your answers to the following questions.

1. Give at least two examples of operating systems.

   _____

2. Describe what object code is.

   _____

   _____

3. Describe the process that the computer goes through to carry out a set of instructions that a programmer has typed into a compiler.

   _____

   _____

4. How does the memory of a computer work?

_____

_____

_____

_____

_____

5. Describe a client/server relationship.

_____

_____

6. What is the most important thing you can do as a student of computer science?

_____

_____

7. What happens when a program is executed?

_____

_____

8. Write an algorithm for getting up in the morning for school.

_____

_____

_____

_____

_____

_____

_____

_____

_____

_____

_____

9. What is the difference between high-level and low-level languages?

_____

_____

_____

_____

10. Why learn C++?

_____

_____

_____

_____

_____

_____

11. List some application software that you have used.

_____

_____

_____

_____

_____

_____

Use the following code to answer the questions below.

```
//    Program file:  divide.cpp
//
//    This program displays the result of dividing two integers

#include <iostream.h>

int main()
{
    int first, second;

    cout << "Enter the first number:  ";
    cin >> first;
    cout << "Enter the second number: ";
    cin >> second;
    cout << "The result of dividing " << first << " by " << second
         << " is " << first / second << endl;
}
```

12. Key this program in and run it using several data points, including one with zero as the second integer. Explain what happens for each run.

_____

_____

_____

_____

_____

13. Edit the program by deleting the comma between first and second in the variable declaration. What happens when you try to run this program now and why?

_____

_____

14. Write a new program that displays the text "Hello world!!" on the terminal screen. Start by creating a new empty file with your editor, and type in the program from scratch.

_____

_____

_____

_____

_____

_____

_____

_____

_____

IN THE LAB

PROJECT 1-1

Find a magazine or newspaper article that discusses something that interests you about the technological world we live in. Cut out the article and write a brief summary of it and why it interests you. Be prepared to share this information with the class.

PROJECT 1-2

Find a website that is related to C++ or another programming language. Describe the website and how you might be able to use it for this course.

PROJECT 1-3

Find out what "object-oriented programming" is and why it is such a hot topic in the field of computer science.

PROJECT 1-4

Describe at least two disciplines (fields of study) that involve computer programming or could potentially involve computer programming. Give details about how these subjects could integrate programming.

PROJECT 1-5

Find out the history of the term "bug" as in "debugging" a program. Describe the term and its origin.

PROJECT 1-6

Interview a computer programmer or systems analyst about her/his job. Be prepared to share your findings with the class.

LESSON 2   PROBLEM-SOLVING FUNDAMENTALS: DATA TYPES AND OUTPUT

FILL IN THE BLANK

Complete the following sentences by writing the word or words in the blanks provided.

1. A(n) _____ is a word that already has a meaning in C++, so it cannot be used as a variable.

2. A(n) _____ is a subdivision of a program that performs a certain task.

3. Each module of a program should be described using_____.

4. Variables, or words that are defined by the programmer, are called _____.

5. Before writing the actual code for a program, it is useful to write out the program in _____, which is a half-English, half-code method.

6. A(n) _____ job is to develop and maintain large software systems.

7. A group of characters is called a(n) _____ in C++.

8. The process of solving a problem by breaking up the task into smaller, more manageable subtasks is called _____.

9. After writing a program, even if it compiles and executes, a programmer should always _____.

10. It is important to put _____ into a program so other programmers will understand the program and its functions.

TRUE/FALSE

Circle T if the statement is true or circle F if the statement is false.

T   F   1. A good programmer will not need to use comments.

T   F   2. The C++ compiler is not case-sensitive (it doesn't matter if you use capital letters or small letters).

T   F   3. Two slash characters (//) will tell the compiler to ignore any statements following.

T   F   4. It is necessary to put a plus sign (+) in front of positive numbers in C++.

T   F   5. It is alright to have numbers in a variable name as long as the number does not come first.

T   F   6. A file called "apstring.h" should be included in the programs written for this class that have variables that represent strings.

T   F   7. "Defining" a problem means developing an algorithm for that problem.

T   F   8. A coordinate grid on which the grid of pixels appears is standard on most computers.

T   F   9. Object-oriented design is one of the most straight forward ways to learn to solve problems with a computer.

T   F   10. A "main program heading" is not necessary in order to run a program.

MULTIPLE CHOICE

Select the best response for the following statements.

1. To represent real numbers, the following data type should be used:
   a. char
   b. double
   c. real
   d. int
   e. None of the above.

2. The word "int" in C++ is a
   a. preprocessor directive.
   b. main program heading.
   c. data type.
   d. format manipulator.
   e. None of the above.

3. Keywords consist of
   a. programmer-supplied identifiers.
   b. library identifiers.
   c. reserved words.
   d. Both b and c.
   e. None of the above.

4. All comments should be made by
   a. preceding with a double slash (//).
   b. putting in quotations.
   c. using a '\n' character sequence.
   d. preceding with a com.

5. The following syntax is correct:
   a. int num= -29,000
   b. int const = 29000
   c. int 29000 = num
   d. int num = 29000
   e. All of the above.

6. To use the tab key, one would have to use the following command:
   a. [tab]
   b. "\tab"
   c. '\t'
   d. "TAB"

7. A variable that holds a value of "Name" must be of data type
   a. double
   b. word
   c. char
   d. string
   e. None of the above.

8. By directing a value into the standard output stream, one will
   a. be able to read values in from the keyboard.
   b. be able to read in strings.
   c. be using top-down design.
   d. produce output on the screen.
   e. None of the above.

SEQUENCE

1. Use numbers 1–6 to show the order in which these sections appear in a program.

   _____ Main program heading

   _____ Declaration section

   _____ Statement section

   _____ Preprocessor directives

   _____ Constant definition section

2. Use the numbers 1–6 to show the order in which the steps that will help develop good problem-solving habits should occur.

   _____ Document the program.

   _____ Run the program.

   _____ Write the code for the program.

   _____ Analyze the problem.

   _____ Test the results.

   _____ Develop an algorithm.

MATCHING

Place the letter of the keystroke on the right that will execute the highlight movement on the left.

_____ 1. comments	a. used to display images on a computer screen
_____ 2. pixels	b. notes written in half-English, half-code
_____ 3. pseudocode	c. notes to be ignored by the compiler
_____ 4. algorithm	d. a diagram made up of symbols used to illustrate an algorithm
_____ 5. structure chart	e. a set of instructions that will help solve a problem.

WRITTEN QUESTIONS

Write your answers to the following questions.

1. List and describe the steps to good programming habits.

_____

_____

_____

_____

_____

_____

_____

_____

_____

_____

2. What is the purpose of documentation in programming?

_____

_____

_____

_____

_____

3. If the program compiles and runs correctly, what is the point of testing it further?

_____

_____

_____

_____

4. Describe the top-down design method of programming.

_____

_____

_____

5. Look at the following code and write down what you think the output of the program would be:

```
#include <iostream.h>
main()
{
 int number = 5
 cout << "This is a number:" << number;
 return 0;
}
```

_____

6. For the code in question 5, describe what "cout" does.

_____

7. What data type is being used in the code for question 5?

_____

8. What information would a programmer need to know before writing a software system that would maintain grades?

_____

_____

_____

_____

_____

9. Why use a "const" definition?

_____

_____

_____

_____

10. Identify any errors in the following definitions and declarations. (Write "none" if there are no errors.)

   a. `1stnum`   _____

   b. `num1`   _____

   c. `first num`   _____

   d. `firstNum`   _____

   e. `A`   _____

   f. `A\X`   _____

   g. `city,state`   _____

   h. `else`   _____

11. Write constant definition statements for the following:
   a. Ten of people in the room. _____
   b. The tax rate in Wisconsin (5.5%). _____
   c. Your name. _____

12. Develop an algorithm that will perform these operations:
   a. $\sqrt{a+b}$

   _____

   _____

   _____

   _____

   _____

   b. $\frac{a}{c} + \frac{b}{d}$

   _____

   _____

   _____

   _____

   _____

   _____

13. What preprocessor directive must be included in order to use the formatting functions?

   _____

14. What preprocessor directive must be included in order to direct a value into the standard output stream?

_____

15. Use the following code to outline the five components of a program.

```
// This program calculates the area of a circle, given its radius.
#include<iostream.h>                    _____
const double PI = 3.14;                 _____
int main()                              _____
{

  double radius, area;                  _____


  cout << "Enter the radius of the circle: ";  _____
  cin >> radius;                        _____
  area = PI*radius*radius;              _____
  cout << "The area is: " << area << endl;  _____
  return 0;                             _____
}
```

16. Identify any errors in the following code:

```
                                        _____

int main                                _____
{
  cout << "This will print to the screen << '\n';  _____
  cout << "Please enter a number: " ;   _____
  cin >> number;                        _____
  cout << "The number is: " << number << endl;  _____
}
```

17. Rewrite in the program for question 16 fixing the errors you found.

_____

_____

_____

_____

_____

_____

_____

_____

_____

_____

18. Identify any errors in the following code:

```cpp
# include "iostream.h"
int main ( )
{
  int 1num, num2, a number;
  cout << 'Enter a number';
  cout << "The number you entered is: " << num2;
  cout << "The end!"
return 0;
}
```

_____

_____

_____

_____

_____

_____

_____

19. Rewrite the code in question 18 and run the program fixing the errors you found. Write down the input and output.

_____

_____

_____

_____

_____

_____

_____

_____

_____

_____

_____

_____

_____

_____

20. Give the output of the following code (using a piece of graph paper, if available):

```cpp
#include <iostream.h>

#include <iomanip.h>

int main()
{
cout << setw(25) << "COMPUTER PROGRAMMING";

cout << endl;

cout << setiosflags(ios::left);

cout << setw(20) << "Name" << setw(5) << "Score:";

cout << endl << endl;

cout << setw(20) <<  "Chris Casper" ;

cout << setw(5) << "98";

cout << endl;

cout << setw(20) <<  "Andy Brady" ;

cout << setw(5) << "89";

cout << endl;

cout << setw(20) <<  "Adam Clark" ;

cout <<  setw(5) << "82";

cout << endl;

cout << setw(20) <<  "Anna Schwarz" ;

cout <<  setw(5) << "100";

cout << endl;

return 0;

}
```

_____

_____

_____

_____

_____

_____

_____

_____

IN THE LAB

PROJECT 2-1

Write a program that prints out your course schedule.

PROJECT 2-2

Write a program that prints a message of your choice to the fourth line of the screen.

PROJECT 2-3

Write a program that prints out a heading for a list of grades for students. For example:

                         Computer Science

    Student Name   Proj1   Proj2   Proj3   Quiz   Average

The course title should be centered in the middle of the screen.
The Student Name should be in the first column and reserve 25 spaces for each name.
The assignment definitions should be spaced five spaces apart.
The Average should start in the 50th column.

LESSON 3   MORE PROBLEM-SOLVING FUNDAMENTALS: CALCULATION AND INPUT

FILL IN THE BLANK

Complete the following sentences by writing the word or words in the blanks provided.

1. The highest integer number that can be stored in a 16-bit machine is _____.

2. When the value of an integer exceeds the amount in #1, a(n) _____ will occur.

3. Values of memory locations that can be changed during the program are called _____.

4. Values that will not be changed are _____.

5. The operator used to give the remainder after dividing is called the _____.

6. The 16-bit area used to hold a single character is called a(n) _____ variable.

7. A group of characters is called a(n) _____ in C++.

8. Integers are stored in _____ notation.

9. To put a value into a memory location, the programmer uses a(n) _____.

10. A person entering values into the program through use of the keyboard is called a(n) _____.

TRUE/FALSE

Circle T if the statement is true or circle F if the statement is false.

T   F   1. When a string is declared, no memory is set aside.

T   F   2. The compiler will temporarily change the data type to fit the calculation being performed.

T   F   3. Storing an extremely small number into a `double float` data type can result in an error in output.

T   F   4. Typecasting will temporarily change the data type for a variable.

T   F   5. Every time the `getline( )` function is used it must be followed up with a `cin.ignore( )`.

T   F   6. The + operator can be used to "add" words together (concatenate).

T   F   7. Compound assignments can be used with strings as well as with integers.

T   F   8. Functions defined in classes are called member functions.

T   F   9. Relative coordinates and absolute coordinates refer to the same thing.

T   F   10. Variables can be declared and initialized in the same statement.

T   F   11. You can initialize multiple variables to the same value in the same statement.

T   F   12. The * operator performs multiplication.

T   F   13. C++ allows you to divide by zero.

T   F   14. The modulus operator is the & sign.

MULTIPLE CHOICE

Select the best response for the following statements.

1. Because programmers often use basic operations in many programs, C++ provides built-in
   a. member functions.
   b. library functions.
   c. assignment statements.
   d. type promotion.
   e. None of the above.

2. When the number 192875 is used in an integer data type the following will occur
   a. cancellation error.
   b. explicit type conversion.
   c. representational error.
   d. integer overflow.
   e. None of the above.

3. Integers are stored in
   a. binary notation.
   b. assignment operators.
   c. parameters.
   d. scientific notation.
   e. Both b and d.

4. Which of the following examples shows the correct way to typecast a variable?
   a. `result (int) = double_value;`
   b. `result = (int) double_value;`
   c. `result = int(double_value);`
   d. `result = double_value (int);`

5. If the variable `result` is defined as type `int` in the expression `result = 26.975 / 2;`, the value placed in result will
   a. be promoted to a double variable.
   b. be typecast to a double variable.
   c. cause an overflow condition.
   d. be truncated.
   e. None of the above.

6. If the variables x and y are defined as integers, and the variables a and b are defined as double, which variable will be promoted when the expression x = (a+ b) * y is processed?
   a. a
   b. b
   c. y
   d. x
   e. None of them

7. Storing an extremely small number in a double data type can result in
   a. overflow.
   b. underflow.
   c. truncation.
   d. promotion.

8. An overflow condition occurs when
   a. a value is too large for its data type.
   b. a decimal value is stored into an integer field.
   c. too many variables are defined in the program.
   d. an integer is divided by a floating point number.

WRITING C++ STATEMENTS

Write a statement that satisfies each of the descriptions below. Do not forget the semicolon.

1. Assign the value of *gross_amount – cost* into a variable called *net*.

   _____

2. Assign the remainder of 16 divided by 3 into the variable *remainder*.

   _____

3. The value of *number* when squared is stored in the variable *squared*. (Use a function from the <math.h> library.

   _____

4. The amount of *cost* times *sales_tax* is stored in the variable *total*.

   _____

5. A third of the product of length, width, and height is stored in volume.

   _____

MATCHING

Place the letter of the keystroke on the right that will execute the highlight movement on the left.

_____ 1. assignment statement

_____ 2. binary arithmetic

_____ 3. library function

_____ 4. member function

_____ 5. parameter

_____ 6. overflow

_____ 7. underflow

_____ 8. implicit type conversion

_____ 9. explicit type conversion

_____ 10. extractor

_____ 11. inserter

a. A value or expression passed in a function call

b. When programmers use typecasts to convert a value to a different type.

c. The operator used to direct output into the output stream

d. The way in which a programmer places a value into a memory location

e. An error that occurs when a number that is too large or beyond the range of its data type definition

f. The operator used to direct input into a variable

g. When the computer temporarily changes that data type of a number in order to perform an operation

h. Functions specific to a particular class

i. Code provided by C++ that will perform basic operations

j. An error that occurs when a very small number is stored as zero

k. The operations performed on integers stored in memory

WRITTEN QUESTIONS

Write your answers to the following questions.

1. Evaluate the following integer expressions:
   a. 19 / 5 _____
   b. −19 / 5 _____
   c. 19 % 5 _____
   d. −19 % 5 _____
   e. (3 + 5) % 28 / 3 _____
   f. 12 + 3 % 17 − 4 _____
   g. (12 + 3) % (17 − 2) _____

2. Explain the difference in how the computer manages memory for string variables and numeric variables.

_____

_____

_____

_____

_____

3. What output will be produced by the following:

    a. `solution = 110/220;`   _____

          `cout << solution;`   _____

    b. `solution = 110.0/220.0;` _____

          `cout << solution;`   _____

4. Look at the following code and write down what you think the output of the program would be:

```
# include <iostream.h>

int main()
{
  int number = 10;
  char letter = 'A';
  cout << "number: " << number << " letter: " << letter <<endl;
  letter = letter + number;
  cout << letter << endl;
  number = number + letter;
  cout << number << endl;
  return 0;
}
```

_____

_____

_____

_____

_____

_____

5. Identify any errors in the following code:

```
#include <iostream.h>              _____
#include <iomanip.h>               _____
#include "apstring.h"              _____

apstring string1, string2;         _____
int number;                        _____
"my name" = string1;               _____
cout << "Enter a number: ";        _____
cin >> number;                     _____
cout << "Enter a  string: ";       _____
cin >> "string2";                  _____
cout << "The strings are: " << "string1"

   << " and " << string2 << " and the number is " << number << endl;
return 0;                          _____
}
```

6. Identify any errors in the following program:

```
#include <iostream.h>          _____
int main( )                    _____
{
  int salary, total_amount, num_years;  _____
  cout << "Enter your salary: ";  _____
  cin >> salary;                 _____
  cout << "Enter the number of years you have worked at this salary: ";
  cin >> num_years;              _____
  total_amount = salary * num_years;  _____
  cout << "You have made $ " << total_amount << " working here!" << endl;
  return 0;                      _____
}
```

7. Identify any errors in the following program:

```
#include <iostream.h>          _____
#include "apstring.h"          _____
#include "math.h"

int main( )                    _____
int age, first_name, quiz1, quiz2, quiz3, average;  _____
apstring last_name;            _____

cout << "Enter your name: ";   _____
cin >> first >> last;          _____
cout << Enter your age: ;      _____
cout << "Enter the three quiz grade with a space separating: ";
                               _____
cin >> quiz1 >> quiz2 >> quiz3;  _____
average = quiz1 + quiz2 + quiz3 / 3;  _____

cout << "Your average so far is: " << average << endl;
                               _____
return 0;                      _____
}
```

8. Identify any errors in the following program:

```
#include <iostream.h>                    _____
int main( )                              _____
{
    int dividend1, divisor1, remainder1;  _____
    double div2, divis2, rem2;            _____
    double anumber;                       _____
    cout << "Enter the first dividend and divisor (space in between): ";
                                          _____
    cin >> dividend1 >> divisor1;         _____
    remainder1 = dividend1 % divisor1;    _____
    cout << "Enter the second dividend and divisor (space in between):";
                                          _____
    cin >> div2 >> divis2, rem2;          _____
    rem2 = div2 % divis2;                 _____
    cout << "The first quotient is: " << dividend1/divisor1 << "with remainder
" << remainder1;                          _____
    cout << endl;                         _____
    cout << "The second quotient is: " << div2/divis2 << "with remainder " <<
rem2;                                     _____

    anumber++;                            _____
cout << "The number is now: " << anumber; _____
}
```

9. Identify the errors in the following code:

```
#include <iostream.h>                     _____
#include <apstring.h>                     _____

int main( )                               _____
{
apstring full_name;                       _____
int grade, gender;                        _____

cout << "Enter the grade you are in: ";   _____
cin >> grade;                             _____
cout << "Enter your full name: ";         _____
getline(cin, full_name);                  _____
cout "Enter your gender:";                _____
cin >> gender;                            _____
return 0;                                 _____
}
```

10. Give the output for this code:

```cpp
#include <iostream.h>
int main( )
{
   int sum = 0;
   int new_number = 5;
   sum = sum + new_number;
   new_number = 10;
   sum = sum + new_number;
   new_number = 7;
   sum = sum + new_number;
   cout << "The sum is " << sum << endl;
return 0;
}
```

_____

11. Give the output for this code:

```cpp
#include <iostream.h>
int main( )
{
   int x = 15, y = 3;
   x +=y;
   cout << x << " " << y;
   return 0;
}
```

_____

IN THE LAB

PROJECT 3-1

Write a program that simulates a *Mad Libs*. That is, this program will tell a story dependent on nouns, verbs, numbers, adjectives, etc. Given by the user.

PROJECT 3-2

Write code that asks the user for his/her name, address, social security number, and salary and then prints this information in a unique format.

PROJECT 3–3

Write code that asks the user to enter a word and gives the length of the word entered.

PROJECT 3-4

Write code that asks the user for a base, present tense verb, then gives the plural, past tense, and present participle (-ing) of that word.

PROJECT 3-5

Write code that asks for the radius of a circle and finds the perimeter and area of that circle.

PROJECT 3-6

Write code that asks for the length and width of a lot and gives the area and perimeter of the lot.

PROJECT 3–7

Write code that calculates the cost of a speeding ticket. The program should ask the user for the speed limit and the actual speed. The ticket should be $35 for the first 5 miles over plus $12.57 for each additional mile over the speed limit.

PROJECT 3-8

A textbook company sells Math books for $37.50 each, English books for $27.75 each, Computer Programming books for $32.80 each, and History books for $35.62 each. Write a program that asks the user how many of each type of book is needed, then calculate the total cost (including tax). A typical input screen would be:

Please enter the number of Math books needed:
Please enter the number of English books needed:
Please enter the number of Computer books needed:
Please enter the number of History books needed:

Thank you!
****

Books-R-Us
October 26, 2000

Quantity	Item	Cost
4	Math books	$150.00
2	English books	$ 55.50
5	Computer Programming books	$164.00
2	History books	$ 71.24
	Subtotal......................................	$440.74
	Tax(.055)......................................	$ 24.24
	Total Sale....................................	$464.98

PROJECT 3-9

Write a program that calculates the distance of the hypotenuse, and gives the length of two sides of a triangle.

LESSON 4   USER-DEFINED FUNCTIONS

FILL IN THE BLANK

Complete the following sentences by writing the word or words in the blanks provided.

1. A(n) _____ is an identifier that is declared before the main block of a program that can be used throughout the entire program.

2. The main function should be coded to return a value of _____ when it completes to indicate to the operating system that the program ended normally.

3. A variable's _____ determines where it is accessible within a program.

4. _____ occur when a change in a non local variable is caused by the misuse of reference parameters or global variables.

5. The _____ is the main function of a program.

6. Data values can be passed from the caller to the function through _____.

7. _____ are functions that do not return a value.

8. A higher level module that can consist of several functions is a(n) _____.

9. Once a function has been declared, a(n) _____ of that function must be written.

10. Using the same function form on different data types is called _____ functions.

TRUE/FALSE

Circle T if the statement is true or F if the statement is false.

T   F   1. Functions should be designed as generally as possible.

T   F   2. If the value of the actual parameter must be changed by the function, declare the formal parameter as a value parameter.

T   F   3. Documentation isn't as necessary for software engineers as it is for beginning programming students.

T   F   4. System designers and programmers often spend half of their time and effort on documentation.

T   F   5. Dividing a program into functions can improve the organization of a program.

T   F   6. One drawback to writing functions in a program is it is more difficult to test and debug the program.

T   F   7. When the end of the statement of a function is reached, the next statement to be executed is the next statement of the main function.

T   F   8. A program does not need functions besides the main function.

T   F   9. A function that is written for one program should not be used in other programs.

T   F   10. The syntax for defining the main function of a program is much different from the syntax for other functions within the program.

T   F   11. All functions must return a value to the function that called it indicating the result of the function's execution.

T   F   12. Functions being used with a program need to be defined at the top of the program by coding a function prototype (function declaration).

T F 13. All functions must contain a return statement even if the function is defined with the void keyword.

T F 14. It is a good idea to declare all or most of your variables as global, so they can be used throughout the program.

T F 15. A library header file defines the functions, but does not implement them.

MULTIPLE CHOICE

Select the best response for the following statements.

1. One function can execute another function by _____ the function.
   a. sending
   b. calling
   c. requesting
   d. declaring
   e. Both a and d.

2. A variable or identifier's _____ determines where it can be accessed by any functions used within a program.
   a. scope
   b. scale
   c. type
   d. priority
   e. Both a and b.
   f. All of the above.

3. Variables that are declared within a specific function are called _____ variables.
   a. function specific
   b. global
   c. private
   d. public
   e. None of the above.

4. Creating a program by defining multiple functions to perform specific tasks makes a program easier to
   a. document
   b. debug
   c. test
   d. execute
   e. Both b and c.

5. Functions that are not going to return any value to the calling function should be defined with the _____ keyword.
   a. null
   b. void
   c. private
   d. noret
   e. None of the above.

6. It is best to use _____ as formal parameters when you do not want the value of the parameter to change after it has been sent to the function.
   a. reference parameters
   b. actual parameters
   c. value parameters
   d. constant reference parameters
   e. None of the above.

7. When the size of the data being sent to a function is relatively large and you do not want the value of the original variable to be changed by the function, it is best to pass it by using a _____.
   a. reference parameter
   b. formal parameter
   c. value parameter
   d. constant reference parameter
   e. Both b and c.

8. When writing a program that will return the area and perimeter of a rectangle, the parameter used should be a _____.
   a. reference parameter
   b. formal parameter
   c. value parameter
   d. constant reference parameter
   e. constant value parameter

9. The following function definition illustrates a function that matches with the function declaration _____.

   ```
   // Function:  getword
   //  Gets a word out of a paragraph.
   //
   //   Input:  An integer that describes the position of the word in the paragraph.
   // Output: The word that occurs at that position.
   ```

   a. apstring getword;
   b. apstring getword(int number);
   c. int getword(apstring word);
   d. int getword( );
   e. None of the above.

10. The following function definition illustrates a function that matches with the function declaration _____.

    ```
    // Function getinfo
    //   Gets the size of the diameter and the height of a cylindrical cone
    //   Input:  Variables for the values of the diameter and height
    // Output: Values for the diameter and height
    ```

    a. getinfo(double diameter, double height);
    b. double getinfo(double diameter, double height);
    c. void getinfo(double &diameter, double &height);
    d. void geting(double diameter, double height);
    e. None of the above

MATCHING

Place the letter of the keystroke on the right that will execute the highlight movement on the left.

_____ 1. A simplified version of a large program that will show if the logic in the larger program will work.

_____ 2. A block of code that is written to perform one subtask.

_____ 3. The section of the program where the identifier can be used.

_____ 4. A program that completes a specific task that can be included in a larger program as if it were a built-in function.

_____ 5. Functions that do not return a value.

_____ 6. The block of code that describes the function including function heading and executable statements.

_____ 7. A type of parameter that sends a value from the caller to the function and will not be changed.

_____ 8. A type of parameter that is used when you want a function to return more than one value.

_____ 9. The parameter(s) used when the function is called.

_____ 10. The parameter(s) name that follows the type in the parameter list of a function heading.

_____ 11. A higher-level module that can consist of several functions.

_____ 12. Identifiers declared before the main block of a program that can be used throughout the entire program.

_____ 13. Identifiers that are restricted to a specific function

_____ 14. An accidental change in a nonlocal variable that is caused by misuse of reference parameters or global variables.

_____ 15. A way of developing functions where the problem solver considers what a function does and gives it a name and sufficient comments to tell the user what it does.

a. void functions

b. actual parameters

c. formal parameters

d. abstract data type

e. global identifier

f. value parameters

g. reference parameters

h. side effects

i. local identifier

j. module

k. scope of an identifier

l. stub programming

m. subprogram

n. implementation

o. procedural abstraction

WRITTEN QUESTIONS

Write your answers to the following questions.

1. Describe situations when you would declare formal parameters as
   a. Value Parameters

   _____

   _____

   b. Reference Parameters

   _____

   _____

   _____

   c. Constant Reference Parameters

   _____

   _____

2. Which of the following are valid function declarations? Explain what is wrong with those that are not.
   a. `cube(double x);`
   b. `void cube(x);`
   c. `void cube(float x);`
   d. `apstring get_word(int num);`
   e. `apstring get_word(apstring word, int num)`

3. Find the errors in the following function declarations:
   a.

   ```
   //Function: Print Heading
   // Prints the heading of a course
   //
   // Inputs: course name
   // Outputs: A heading for the course
   void PrintHeading(name);
   ```

   b.

   ```
   // Function getName
   // Promps the user for a name
   //
   // Inputs: A string representing the name
   // Outputs: The name the user entered
   apstring getName(apstring name);
   ```

   c.

   ```
   //  Function: cube
   // Cubes a number
   //
   //  Input: A double number
   // Output: The cube of that number
   int cube (double number);
   ```

4. What is the purpose of the void keyword in a function declaration statement? Does using the void keyword result in any difference in that function's structure?

_____

_____

_____

_____

5. Describe the difference between global and local variables. Give examples of when you would use them.

_____

_____

_____

_____

_____

_____

_____

_____

6. What is a parameter?

_____

_____

7. What are two ways in which values can be returned from a function?

_____

_____

_____

8. Find the errors in the following code:

```
#include <iostream.h>
#include <apstring.h>
apstring name;
//Function:  getName
// This function gets a name from the user
//
// Input: none.
// Output: the name entered
apstring getName(apstring &name);
intmain()
{
    apstring thisname;
    getName(thisname);
    cout << thisname;
return 0;
}
```

```
apstring getName(apstring &name)
{
    cout << "Enter a name: ";
    cin >> name;
    return name;
}
```

9. Find the errors in the following code:

```
#include <iostream.h>

double getinfo(double &diam, double &height)
intmain()
{
    int d, h;
    getinfo(d,h);
    cout << "diameter is: " << d << " and height is: " << h;
return 0;
}
double getinfo(double diam, double height)
{
    cout << "Enter the diameter: " ;
    cin >> diam;
    cout << "Enter the height: ";
    cin >> height;
}
```

10. Write code that will implement the following function:

```
// Function: happy
// This function prints the lyrics to the song, "Happy Birthday to You" to a
specified person
//
// Input: A name of a person
// Output: The song
```

_____

_____

_____

_____

_____

_____

11. Write code that will implement the following function definition:

```
// Function: Cost
// This function returns the cost of an item
//
// Input: The price of the item and the amount of tax
// Output: Cost with tax
```

12. Write code that will implement the following function definition:

```
// Function:    dimensions
// This function asks the user for the length and width of a rectangle
//
// Input:  Variables in which to store the length and width values
// Output: none
```

13. Write code that will implement the following function definition:

```
// Function: perimeter
// This function calculates the perimeter of a rectangle
//
// Input: The length and width of a rectangle
// Output: The perimeter of the rectangle.
```

14. What is the output for the following program?

```cpp
#include <iostream.h>
#include "apstring.h"

void hada(apstring animal);
void witha(apstring sound);
void mainVerse();

main()
{
    mainVerse();

    hada("cow");
    witha("moo");
    mainVerse();
    return 0;
}

void mainVerse()
{
    cout << "Old McDonald had a farm ";
    cout << endl << "And on his farm he had a ";
}

void hada(apstring animal)
{
 cout << animal << endl;
}

void witha(apstring sound)
{
    cout << "with a " << sound << " " << sound << " here and a " << endl;
    cout << sound << " " << sound << " there. Here a " << sound << " there a
" << sound << endl;
    cout << "everywhere a " << sound << " " << sound << endl;

}
```

15. How could you modify the main section of the program above to include verses for a dog and a chicken?

16. How could you combine the `hada` and `witha` functions into one function called verse that would still print out the same song?

17. The following program will run when compiled, but is very poorly written. Identify its weaknesses and change them to produce a better program.

```
// Program file:  circle.cpp
//  This program computes the area of a circle.
// The user is prompted for the value of the radius and the program displays
the area.

#include <iostream.h>
#include <math.h>
```

```cpp
// global data
double PI , radius, area;

// Function: print_results
// Displays the area of the circle
//
// Input: real numbers representing the radius and area of a circle
// output: none
void print_results();

// Function: get_data
// This function obtains input from the user for the radius of a circle
//
// Input: none
// Output: a real number representing the radius of a circle

void get_data();

// Function: compute_area
// computes the area of the circle
//
// Input: a real number representing the radius of a circle
// Output: the area of the circle

void compute_area();

intmain()
{
    PI = 3.1416;
    get_data();
    compute_area();
    print_results();
    return 0;
}

void print_results()
{
    cout << "The area is " << area << endl;
}

void get_data()
{
    cout << "Enter the radius of the circle: ";
    cin >> radius;
}
void compute_area()
{
    area = PI*radius*radius;
}
```

18. Identify the errors in the following code:

```
#include <iostream.h>
const double PI = 3.1416;

intmain()
{
   cout << "Enter the radius: ";
    cin >> radius;
    area = radius*radius*PI;
    print_results(area, radius);
return 0;
}

void print_results(double rad, double a)
{
    cout << "The radius is:" << rad << endl;
    cout << "The area is: " << a << endl;
}
```

IN THE LAB

PROJECT 4-1

The following program computes the roots of a quadratic equation. It decomposes the problem into sub problems that are solved with functions. Each function is implemented as a sub. Write the implementations for each function.

```cpp
//  Program file: roots.cpp

//  This program computes the roots of a quadratic equation.
//  The user is prompted for values of a, b, and c, and the
//  program displays the two roots.

#include <iostream.h>
#include <math.h>

//  Function: print_results
//  Displays the roots of a quadratic equation
//
//  Inputs: the two roots of a quadratic equation

void print_results(double root1, double root2);

//  Function: get_data
//  This function obtains inputs from the user for the quadratic equation
//
//  Outputs: three real numbers to use in computing the roots

void get_data(double &a, double &b, double &c);

//  Function: quadratic_roots
//  This function computes the roots of a quadratic equation
//
//  Inputs: three real numbers to use in computing the roots
//  Outputs: the two roots of a quadratic equation

void quadratic_roots(double a, double b, double c, double &root1, double
&root2);

int main()
{
double a, b, c, root1, root2;

get_data(a,b,c);
quadratic_roots(a,b,c,root1,root2);
print_results(root1, root2);
return 0;
}
```

```
void print_results(double root1, double root2)
{
cout << "calling print_results function" << endl;
}

void get_data(double &a, double &b, double &c)
{
cout << "calling get_data function" << endl;
}

void quadratic_roots(double a, double b, double c, double &root1, double
&root2)
{
cout << "calling quadratic_roots function"<< endl;
}
```

PROJECT 4-2

Write a program that will find the area and perimeter of a triangle and rectangle. Include at least four functions.

PROJECT 4-3

Write a program that will calculate the distance between two points (x1, y1) and (x2, y2). For example, the distance between (4,7) and (-2,3) is the square root of 52 or 7.21.

PROJECT 4-4

Write a function to get the determinant of the quadratic equation. Remember the determinant of a quadratic equation is the result of $b^2 - 4 * a * c$.

A sample display for getting input is:

Enter coefficients a, b, and c for the quadratic equation $ax^2 + bx + c = 0$.

a = _____

b = _____

c = _____

Your program should have at least two functions other than the main function.

The program should also include a test in the main function that will test three data sets as follows:

    a. $b^2 - 4ac = 0$ Actual coefficients used to test: a _____ b _____ c _____

    b. $b^2 - 4ac > 0$ Actual coefficients used to test: a _____ b _____ c _____

    c. $b^2 - 4ac < 0$ Actual coefficients used to test: a _____ b _____ c _____

PROJECT 4-5

The Natural Pine Furniture Company has recently hired you to help them convert their antiquated payroll system to a computer-based model. They know you are still learning, so all they want right now is a program that will print a one-week pay report for three employees. You should use the constant definition section for the following:

    a. Federal withholding tax rate   18%

    b. State withholding tax rate   4.5%

    c. Hospitalization $25.65

    d. Union dues $7.85

Each line of input will contain the employee's initials, the number of hours worked and the employee's hourly rate. Your output should include a report for each employee and a summary report for the company files. A sample employee form follows:

Employee:	Spencer
Hours worked:	40.00
Hourly rate:	9.75
Total wages	390.00
Deductions:	
Federal withholding	70.20
State withholding	17.55
Hospital	26.65
Union Dues	<u>7.85</u>
Total deductions	267.75

Output for a summary report could be:

Natural Pine Furniture Company

Weekly Summary

Gross wages:	$1298.76
Deductions:	
Federal Withholding:	$210.42
State Withholding:	54.00
Hospitalization:	84.23
Union Dues	22.76
Total deductions	371.41
Net Wages	927.35

PROJECT 4-6

The Holiday-Out Motel Company, Inc., wants a program that will print a statement for each overnight customer. Each line of input will contain room number (integer), number of nights stayed (integer), room rate (real), telephone charges (real), and restaurant charges (real). You should use the constant definition section for the date and current tax rate. Each customer statement should include all input data, the date, tax rate and amount, total due, appropriate heading, and appropriate closing message. Test your program by running it for at least two customers. The tax rate applies only to the room cost. A typical input screen is:

Room number:	135
Room rate:	39.95
Number of nights:	3
Telephone charges:	3.75
Meals:	57.50

A customer statement form is:

%%

Holiday Out Motel Company, Inc.

xx-xx-xx (date)

%%

Room number:	135
Room Rate:	$39.95
Number of Nights:	3
Room Cost:	119.85
Tax 5.5%	6.59
Subtotal:	$126.44
Telephone:	3.75
Meals:	57.50
TOTAL DUE	$187.69

%%

THANK YOU FOR STAYING

AT

HOLIDAY-OUT

%%

LESSON 5   SELECTION STATEMENTS

FILL IN THE BLANKS

Complete the following sentences by writing the word or words in the blanks provided.

1. A(n) _____ is one that evaluates to true (1) or false (0).

2. When comparing two values, a(n) _____ is used.

3. Placing a(n) _____ at the end of an if statement's expression can cause an unexpected result.

4. The code within a switch structure must be enclosed in _____.

5. Placing the keyword _____ at the end of each case statement can terminate switch structure processing.

6. If more than one if or if...else statements is used in another if or if...else statement in a program, this is considered a(n) _____.

7. When only one statement of several can be true at a time, the statements are said to be _____ and it is best to use if...else statements rather than separate if statements.

8. An alternative to using nested and extended if statements when using original data is using _____ statements that also allow for multiple selection.

9. Only _____ (those we have studied except for `apstring` and `double`) may be used in a switch statement.

10. To avoid a crash by dividing by 0, you can make a(n) _____, which will check the condition first and print an error message if the expectation of that statement is not met.

TRUE/FALSE

Circle T if the statement is true or F if the statement is false.

T   F   1. Relational operators cannot be used with strings.

T   F   2. C++ is the only programming language with an if structure.

T   F   3. You must always use braces when creating if structures.

T   F   4. If/else structures using ordinal data can be replaced by a switch structure.

T   F   5. An if structure executes the code that is part of the structure when the if expression evaluates to true.

T   F   6. Relational and arithmetic operators serve the same purpose.

T   F   7. An if statement should be immediately followed by a semicolon.

T   F   8. A robust program is a very large program.

T   F   9. The C++ structure that uses a case label is the switch structure.

T   F   10. The selector in a case statement can have any of the data types we have studied so far.

MULTIPLE CHOICE

Select the best response for the following statements.

1. Decision-making structures in C++ are called _____ structures.
   a. branching
   b. control
   c. sequence
   d. selection
   e. switch

2. Which of the following shows the symbols that must surround a block of code for an if structure?
   a. { }
   b. ( )
   c. [ ]
   d. : :
   e. \

3. Which of the following expression does NOT compare values?
   a. if (x == 2)
   b. if (x = 2)
   c. if (x >= 2 && y <= 3)
   d. if !(x > 2)
   e. All of the above compare value.

4. The _____ keyword can be used within a switch structure to execute specific code if no other conditions are matched.
   a. continue
   b. break
   c. other
   d. default
   e. None of the above.

5. Which of the following is an invalid case expression?
   a. case "CAT":
   b. case 'A':
   c. case "A":
   d. case 25:
   e. Both a and c.

6. A program that protects against possible crashes is said to be _____.
   a. robust
   b. clean
   c. tight
   d. logical
   e. None of the above.

7. An if statement is an example of a(n) _____ selection.
   a. one-way
   b. two-way
   c. multiway
   d. Both a and c
   e. None of the above

8. An expression that returns a value of true (1) or false (0) is a(n) _____ expression.
   a. Boolean
   b. True-false
   c. relational
   d. nested
   e. Both b and c.

MATCHING

Place the letter of the keystroke on the right that will execute the highlight movement on the left.

_____ 1. A complete expression that uses logical connectives and negations to generate Boolean values.

_____ 2. The use of the NOT logical operator (!) with a Boolean expression that returns true or false.

_____ 3. An expression in which two values are compared using a single relational operator.

_____ 4. Comments that state what you expect to happen to an under certain circumstances.

_____ 5. Several statements grouped together in braces.

_____ 6. A selection statement used within another selection statement.

_____ 7. Operators that compare data items of the same type.

_____ 8. Statements that allow the computer to make a decision.

_____ 9. A statement with a value of true or false.

_____ 10. The state in which a program is "fool proof" or protected against possible crashes and "bad" data.

a. Boolean statement

b. Simple Boolean expression

c. Assertion

d. Compound Boolean

e. Compound statement

f. Negation

g. Nested if statement

h. Robust

i. Selection statement

j. Relational operator

WRITTEN QUESTIONS

Write your answers to the following questions.

1. What are the six relational operators and what symbols are used to represent each one?

   _____

   _____

   _____

   _____

   _____

   _____

   _____

2. Describe how the logical AND (&&) operator works and give an example of its use. Give one example that will return a value of true and one that will return a value of false.

   _____

   _____

   _____

   _____

3. What is the purpose of the logical not operator? Give examples of its use, one that will return a true, and another that will return a false.

   _____

   _____

   _____

4. If x = 2, y = 8, and z = 12, what would the expression (x!= 2 && (y >=9 | | z ==12) evaluate to, and why? What would the expression (x!= 2 | | y >=9 | | z ==12) evaluate to, and why?

   _____

   _____

   _____

5. In the program below, each cout statement is numbered. Beside each of the numbered statements, indicate what output the statement will produce.

```cpp
#include <iostream.h>

int main()
{
 int b = 5, i = 8, j = 0;
 bool yesNo;

 yesNo = (!(b <=i) && (b <= 5));      //1 _____
 cout << yesNo << endl;

 yesNo = ! yesNo;
 cout << yesNo << endl;               //2 _____

 yesNo = (b < i && j < i);
  if(yesNo == 1)
  yesNo = 0;
  cout << yesNo << endl;             //3 _____

if(b>i && i>j)
  yesNo = 1;
cout << yesNo << endl;               //4 _____

if(yesNo != 0)
  yesNo = 1;
cout<< yesNo << endl;                //5 _____

 return 0;
}
```

6. Identify the errors in this code:

```cpp
// if a is a positive number print the number to the screen and add 10 to it.
if (a >= 0)
     cout << a << endl;
     a = a + 10;
else
     cout << a << " is negative" << endl;
```

7. Identify the errors in this code:

```cpp
intmain( )
{
    int num;
    char grade;
    cout << enter a number;
    cin >> num;

    switch(num);

     case "90": grade = 'A';
                            break;
     case 80:    grade == 'B';
   break;
       case 70:    grade = 'C';
   break;
case 60:                         grade = 'D';
   break;
default:                         grade = 'F';
   break;
```

IN THE LAB

PROJECT 5-1

Given three integers, write a program to print only the largest.

PROJECT 5-2

The Mapes Railroad Corporation pays an annual bonus as part of its profit sharing plan. This year all employees who have been with the company for ten years or more receive a bonus of 12 percent of their annual salary, and those who have worked at Mapes from five through nine years will receive a bonus of 5.75 percent. Those who have been with the company less than five years receive no bonus.

Given the initials of an employee, the employee's annual salary, and the number of years employed with the company, write a program to find and print the bonus. All bonuses are rounded to the nearest dollar. Output should be in the following form:

                    MAPES RAILROAD CORP

    Employee xxx

    Years of Service: nn

    Bonus earned: $yyyy

PROJECT 5-3

The Caswell Catering and Convention Service has asked you to write a computer program to produce customers' bills. The program should read in the following information:

Number of adults to be served
Number of children to be served
Type of meal (Deluxe or Standard)
The room (A, B, C, D, or E prices described below)
The amount of a deposit (if any) to be deducted from the bill

The following charges will be assessed:

For adults, the deluxe meal will cost $15.80 per person and the standard meals will cost $11.75 per person, dessert included. Children's meals will cost 60 percent of adult meals. Everyone within a given party must be served the same meal type.

There are five banquet halls. Room A rents for $55.00, room B rents for $75.00, room C rents for $85.00, room D rents for $100.00, and room E rents for $130.00. The Caswells are considering increasing the room fees in about six months and this should be taken into account.

A surcharge, currently 7 percent, is added to the total bill if the catering is to be done on a weekend (Friday, Saturday, or Sunday).

All customers will be charged the same rate for tip and tax, currently 18 percent. It is only applied to the cost of food.

To persuade customers to pay promptly, a discount is offered if payment is made within 10 days. This discount depends on the amount of the total bill. If the bill is less than $100.00, the discount is .5 percent; if the bill is at least $100 but less than $400 the discount is 3 percent; if the bill is at least $400 but less than $800.00 the discount is 4 percent; and, if the bill is at least $800.00 the discount is 5 percent.

Test your program on each of the following three customers:

Customer A: This customer is using room C on Tuesday night. The party includes 80 adults and 6 children. The standard meal is being served. The customer paid a $60.00 deposit. The total bill payment was made within 10 days.

Customer B: This customer is using room A on Saturday night. Deluxe meals are being served to 15 adults. A deposit of $50.00 was paid. The total bill payment was made within 30 days.

Customer C: This customer is using room D on Sunday afternoon. The party includes 30 children and 2 adults, all of whom are served the standard meal. The total bill payment was made that day.

PROJECT 5-4

Community Hospital needs a program to compute and print a statement for each patient.

Charges for each day are as follows:

room charges: private room, $125.00; semiprivate room, $95.00; ward, $75.00
telephone charge: $1.75
television charge: $3.50

Write a program to get a line of data from the keyboard, compute the patient's bill, and print an appropriate statement. Typical input is

    5PNY

where 5 indicates the number of days spent in the hospital, P represents the room type (P,S, or W), N represents the telephone option (Y or N), and Y represents the television option (Y or N). A statement for the data given follows:

Community Hospital
Patient Billing Statement

Number of days in hospital:	5
Type Room:	Private
Room charge:	$625.00
Telephone charge	$0.00
Television charge	$17.50
TOTAL DUE:	$642.50

Hint: When reading in the string of characters representing the code:

apstring code;
code[0] represents the room number. To convert this to an integer code[0] – '0' will work.
code[1] represents the room type
code[2] represents the telephone option and
code[3] represents the television option.

LESSON 6   REPETITION STATEMENTS

FILL IN THE BLANK

Complete the following sentences by writing the word or words in the blanks provided.

1. Repeating the same task many times is done by using _____ in computer programming.

2. The _____ is the first parameter in the heading of a for loop.

3. The _____ is the part of the heading of a for loop that will cause the loop to stop executing when its value becomes false.

4. Placing a(n) _____ after the ending parenthesis of a for loop will prevent the body of the loop from executing.

5. Multiple statements to be executed within a for loop must be enclosed in _____.

6. A(n) _____ tests a control expression at the beginning of a loop and executes as long as the condition is true.

7. The do-while loop evaluates the control expression at the _____ of the loop.

8. A switch statement discontinues the loop process by using the _____ keyword within the statement.

9. A loop contained within another loop is a(n) _____.

TRUE/FALSE

Circle T if the statement is true or F if the statement is false.

T   F   1. In a for loop, the counter variable is initialized in the heading.

T   F   2. In order for a loop to iterate by some number other than one, the control expression must be modified.

T   F   3. Braces are required for loops that include more than one statement.

T   F   4. A for loop can only have one statement within the loop.

T   F   5. A standard while loop tests the control expression at the end of the loop.

T   F   6. A while loop can be used to replace a for loop.

T   F   7. The break statement causes the loop to begin the next iteration.

T   F   8. Loop structures repeatedly execute the same block of code.

T   F   9. Each pass a program makes through a loop is called a cycle.

T   F   10. The first parameter in a for loop definition initializes the loop's counter variable.

T   F   11. The counter variable in a for loop can only be incremented or decremented by one each pass through the loop.

T   F   12. A while loop executes as long as the counter variable is greater than or equal to zero.

T   F   13. A loop that continues to execute continuously due to an error in programming logic is called an infinite loop.

T   F   14. A do-while loop differs from a while loop in that it tests the condition at the end of the loop.

T   F   15. The continue keyword is used in place of the break statement in a while or do-while loop.

MULTIPLE CHOICE

Select the best response for the following statements.

1. A for loop is an example of a(n) _____ structure.
   a. iteration
   b. repetitive
   c. multiple-pass
   d. continuous
   e. None of the above.

2. The C++ for loop structure includes three _____ contained within parentheses that control the processing of the loop.
   a. initializers
   b. qualifiers
   c. parameters
   d. arguments
   e. None of the above.

3. The difference between a while loop and a for loop is
   a. the while loop executes while a condition is false and the for loop executes while it is true
   b. the while loop executes while a condition is true and the for loop executes while it is false
   c. the for loop requires the programmer to know ahead of time how many iterations will be made and the while loop does not
   d. the while loop tests a condition at the beginning of the loop and the for loop does not
   e. Both b and c.

4. The difference between a while loop and a do-while loop is
   a. the while loop executes while a condition is false; the do while executes while it is true
   b. the do while loop executes while a condition is false, the while executes while it is true
   c. the while loop does not use a counter; the do while does use a counter
   d. the while loop tests the condition at the beginning of the loop; the do while at the end
   e. All of the above.

5. A do-while loop will always
   a. execute the code block at least twice
   b. execute the code block at least once
   c. run until its counter reaches -1
   d. run until its counter reaches 0
   e. both a and c
   f. none of the above

6. The _____ keyword is used to skip an iteration of a loop and start again with the next iteration.
   a. break
   b. skip
   c. bypass
   d. continue
   e. None of the above.

MATCHING

Place the letter of the keystroke on the right that will execute the highlight movement on the left.

_____ **1.** a loop within a loop

_____ **2.** an iteration structure that repeats a statement or group of statements as long as a control expression is true

_____ **3.** a single loop or pass through a group of statements

_____ **4.** the expression in a for loop that changes the counter variable

_____ **5.** programming structures that repeat a group of statements one or more times

_____ **6.** an expression that initializes the counter variable in a for loop

_____ **7.** an iteration structure that repeats a statement or group of statements as long as a control expression is true at the end of the loop

_____ **8.** an iteration structure that repeats one or more statements a specified number of times

_____ **9.** an iteration structure in which iterations continue indefinitely

a. Update expression

b. do while loop

c. for loop

d. indefinite loop

e. initializing expression

f. iteration

g. iteration structures

h. nested loop

i. while loop

WRITTEN QUESTIONS

Write your answers to the following questions.

1. How many times will the loop below iterate?

```
j = 0;
while ( j < 50)
{
     cout << "Hello" << endl;
     ;++;
}
```

_____

2. How many times will the loop below iterate?

```
j = 25;
while (j < = 10 || j >= 25)
{
     cout << "temporary variable is " << j << endl;
     j++;
}
```

_____

3. How many times will the loop below iterate?

```
int x = 5, y = 12;
while(x <= 5 && y >= 0)
{
     x--;
     y = y - x;
}
```

4. What will the output for the following program look like?

```
#include <iostream.h>
intmain( )
{
     int i = 0, j = 0;

     while (i <= 3)
     {
       for(j = 0; j <= 2; j++)
       cout << i << " " << j << endl;
     i++;
     }
return 0;
}
```

5. What output will be produced from the following code:

```
#include <iostream.h>
intmain( )
{
     for(int i = 0; i < 2; i++)
   for (int j = 0; j <= 2; j++)
       for (int k = 3; k > 0; k—)
           cout << i << " " << j << " " << k << endl;
return 0;
}
```

_____

_____

_____

_____

_____

_____

_____

_____

_____

_____

_____

_____

_____

_____

_____

_____

6. What output would be produced by the following program:

```cpp
#include <iostream.h>
intmain( )
{
    int count = 0;
 int sum = 0;

while(count <= 3)
{
  count++;
  sum += count;
  cout << "The sum at this stage is: " << sum << endl;
}

cout << "The count now is " << count << endl;
return 0;
}
```

_____

_____

_____

_____

_____

_____

_____

_____

7. What output will be produced by this code:

```cpp
#include <iostream.h>
intmain( )
{
    int a = 1;
 do
 {
  cout << a << " " << 17%a << endl;
  a = a+1;
 } while (17%a != 5);

 return 0;
}
```

_____

_____

_____

_____
_____
_____
_____

8. What output will be produced by this code:

```cpp
#include <iostream.h>
intmain( )
{
    int a = 5;
 int b = 0;

 while (a > b)
 {
  cout << a << endl;

  do
  {
      cout << a << " " << b << " " << a+b << endl;
      a = a - 2;
  }while (a > 2);

  b = b+2;
 }
cout << endl << "done" << endl;

 return 0;

}
```

_____
_____
_____
_____
_____
_____
_____

9. Identify errors in the following code:

```
int count = 0;
for(k=-5, k<=5, k++)
    if(k%3 = 0)
    {
        cout << "k = " << k << "output";
        while(count < 10)
            count++;
            cout << count << endl;
         count = 0;
    }
```

10. Give the output of the segment of code below, if the following input is given:

Enter the amount of a check, or –999 to quit: $ 123.75

Enter the amount of a check, or –999 to quit: $ 42.50

Enter the amount of a check, or –999 to quit: $ 5.25

Enter the amount of a check, or –999 to quit: $ 23.42

Enter the amount of a check, or –999 to quit: $ -999

```
#include <iostream.h>
intmain( )
{
    double sum = 0.00;
    double amount;

    cout << "Enter the amount of a check, or -999 to quit: $ ";
    cin >> amount;
    while(amount != -999)
    {
      sum = sum + amount;
      cout << "Enter the amount of a check, or -999 to quit: $ ";
      cin >> amount;
    }
    cout << "The monthly total is $ " << sum << endl;
    return 0;
}
```

_____

_____

11. Rewrite the following code using a while loop instead of a do-while loop.

```cpp
#include <iostream.h>

intmain()
{
 double num, squared;
 do
 {
  cout << "Enter a number (0 to quit): ";
  cin >> num;

  squared = num *num;
  cout << num << " squared is " << squared << endl;
 }while (num !=0);
}
```

_____

_____

_____

_____

_____

_____

_____

_____

_____

_____

_____

_____

_____

_____

_____

_____

_____

_____

Use the following program to answer questions 12 – 16

```cpp
// Program file: check.cpp

// This program computes and displays the sum of the checks written
// for a month. The user inputs dollar amounts or the sentinel value
// -999 to quit. If a dollar amount is less than zero (other than the
// sentinel value), the program displays an error message and continues
// to take input.

#include <iostream.h>
#include <iomanip.h>
#include <float.h>

const int SENTINEL = -999;

// Function: get_data
// Gets valid input from user, including a sentinel value
//
// Inputs: lower bound,upper bound of valid input and SENTINEL
// Output: valid input value entered by user

double get_valid_data(double lower_bound, double upper_bound);

int main()
{
 double amount, sum;

 sum = 0.00;
 amount = get_valid_data(0, DBL_MAX - sum);
 while (amount != SENTINEL)
 {
  sum = sum + amount;
  amount = get_valid_data(0, DBL_MAX - sum);
 }
 cout << setiosflags(ios::fixed | ios::showpoint) << setprecision(2);
 cout << "The total amount of checks = $" << sum << endl;
 return 0;
}

double get_valid_data(double lower_bound, double upper_bound)
{
 double data;

 do
 {
  cout << "Enter the amount of a check or -999 to halt: $";
  cin >> data;
```

```
    if ((data != -999) && (data < 0))
        cout << "ERROR: check amount must be at least $0.00 "<< endl;
    else if (data > upper_bound)
        cout << "ERROR: check amount is too large." << endl;
} while ((data != -999) && ((data < 0) || (data > upper_bound)));
return data;
}
```

12. Compile program and run it several times with small dollar amount greater than 0. Make sure you completely understand what the program is doing.

_____

_____

13. Run the program with an initial value of –999. Does the program produce reasonable output?

_____

14. Run the program with two consecutive negative inputs (other than –999), and then a legitimate dollar amount. Does the program behave as expected?

_____

15. Why do you think a while loop is preferred to a do...while loop for the main program loop?

_____

_____

_____

_____

16. Explain why the upper bound on valid input is computed to be DBL_MAX – sum on each iteration of the main loop.

_____

_____

_____

Use the code for the program skipline.cpp to answer questions 17 – 20.

```
// Program file: skipline.cpp

// This program prompts the user for the number of lines to be
// skipped, outputs the number of carriage returns desired,
// and displays a parting message.

#include <iostream.h>
```

```
int main( )
{
 int num_lines;

 cout << "Enter the number of lines to be skipped: ";
 cin >> num_lines;
 for (int i = 1; i <= num_lines; ++i)
  cout << endl;
 cout << "Have a nice day. " << endl;
 return 0;
}
```

17. Compile and run the program with input values 0, 1, and 2, and describe the output. Does the program behave as you would have expected?

_____

18. Modify the program by replacing the <= operator in the loop heading with the < operator. Test the program again with inputs 0, 1, and 2. Explain the error.

19. Modify the program by inserting a while loop that will allow the user to run it as often as s/he wishes.

_____

_____

_____

_____

_____

_____

_____

_____

_____

_____

_____

_____

_____

_____

20. Rewrite the loop heading so that the loop correctly accomplishes the program's task by counting down instead of up.

_____

_____

_____

_____

IN THE LAB

PROJECT 6-1

Write a program that asks the user for a series of integers one at a time. When the user enters the integer 0, the program displays the following information:

    a. the number of integers in the series (not including zero)
    b. the average of the integers
    c. the largest integer in the series
    d. the smallest integer in the series
    e. the difference between the largest and smallest integer in the series

PROJECT 6-2

Write a program that will function as a point-of-sale system at a sports arena snack bar. The snack bar sells only six different items: a sandwich, chips, pickle, brownie, regular drink, and a large drink. All items are subject to sales tax. Set prices for the products.

The program should repeatedly display the menu below until the sale is totaled. The program should keep a running total of the amount of the sale based on costs that you place in constants for each of the food items. The running total should be displayed somewhere on the screen each time the menu is displayed again.

> S – Sandwich
> C – Chips
> B – Brownie
> R – Regular Drink
> L – Large Drink
> X – Cancel and start over
> T – Total the sale

If the sale is canceled, clear your running total and display the menu again. When the sale is totaled, calculate the sales tax based on your local tax rate (use 6% if you have no sales tax in your area). Print the final total due on the screen.

You can use your own functions to design a solution to the problem. You are required to use a function to calculate the sales tax.

PROJECT 6-3

Poynette Tree Service, Inc., offers the following services and rates to its customers:

    a. Tree removal: $500.00 per tree

    b. Tree trimming: $80.00 per hour

    c. Stump grinding $25.00 plus $2.00 per inch for each stump whose diameter exceeds ten inches. No $2.00 charge will be assessed if the diameter is ten inches or less.

Write a complete program to allow the manager, Mr. Woellner, to provide an estimate when he bids on a job. He should be able to run the program as many times as necessary. Your output should include a listing of each separate charge and total. A 10% discount is given for any job whose total exceeds $1000.00. Typical data for one customer are:

    Removal: 7

    Trimming hours 6.5

    Diameter of Stump to grind: 12"

    Typical output for this program would be:

    Poynette Tree Service ,Inc.

Tree Removal:	$3500.00
Trimming:	$ 520.00
Stump Grinding:	$ 29.00
Subtotal:	$ 4049.00
10% Discount (over $1000)	- 404.90
TOTAL..$ 3644.10	

PROJECT 6-4

The prime factorization of a positive integer is the positive integer written as the product of primes. For example, the prime factorization of 72 is

$$72 = 2 * 2 * 2 * 3 * 3$$

Write a program that allows the user to enter a positive integer and then displays the prime factorization of the integer.

LESSON 7   FILES

FILL IN THE BLANK

Complete the following sentences by writing the word or words in the blanks provided.

1. A(n) _____ is a holding place for data.

2. The standard operator, called the _____, is used to send data into the data stream.

3. Files are stored as data structures on a(n) _____.

4. Programs that use the output stream processing and can be written on one hardware system and transported to another are considered _____.

5. Information not relevant to the process in which the operations on ouput streams are performed is considered _____.

6. _____ is the standard operator used to receive data items from the data stream.

7. A statement used to attempt to read an initial datum from the file before using the fail function is called a _____.

8. When passing file streams to a function, they should be passed _____.

9. A search that begins at the first data item, examines it, and continues to read each following data item until a match is found is a(n) _____.

10. A(n) _____ is a channel used to pass data from a sender to a receiver.

TRUE/FALSE

Circle T if the statement is true or F if the statement is false.

T   F   1. If you open a file for output, and that file name already exists on disk, you will receive a warning message.

T   F   2. When writing data to a file the <- operator is used rather than the <<, as is used when writing data to the screen.

T   F   3. A file stream should be opened before using it and closed after using it.

T   F   4. The extractor can be used to detect the end of file by placing it in a loop control condition.

T   F   5. Character data can be read from an input stream by using the put function.

T   F   6. A single file stream can be used to perform reads and writes on multiple files.

MULTIPLE CHOICE

Select the best response for the following statements.

1. Which of the following statements shows the correct method for declaring a file stream for an output file?
   a. opstream outfile;
   b. outfile opstream;
   c. outfile ofstream;
   d. ofstream outfile;
   e. All of the above statements are valid

2. The correct syntax for opening a file stream called `infile`, for the purpose of reading the file, is shown by which of the following statements?
   a. `open.infile("myfile");`
   b. `infile.open("myfile");`
   c. `outfile.open("myfile");`
   d. `infile.open(myfile);`
   e. `open.infile(myfile);`

3. Which of the following statements will write string data to an output stream called outfile?
   a. `outfile << string1 << endl;`
   b. `getline(outfile, string1);`
   c. `outfile >> string1 >> endl;`
   d. `outfile.put(string1);`
   e. `outfile.put << string1;`

Consider the following program code segment for questions 4 and 5:

```
outGoing << dataVal << otherDataVal;
```

4. Because the input and output processes are abstracted, the identifier called `outGoing` could represent which of the following?
       I. Output to the screen.
       II. Output to hard drive file.
       III. Output to floppy drive file.
   a. a only
   b. b only
   c. a and b only
   d. b and c only
   e. a, b, and c

5. The operator `<<` is called an "insertion" operator because of which of the following?
   a. This operator "inserts" data into a data stream.
   b. This operator "inserts" data into the variable called `outGoing`.
   c. This operator "inserts" data into one of the variables given – either `dataVal` or `otherDataVal`.
   d. This operator "inserts" data from an open disk file.
   e. This operator "inserts" data from a console data stream.

Use the following code segment for questions 6 and 7:

```
ifstream infile;
int count = 0;
double num, sum = 0.0;
infile.open("myfile.dat");
infile >> num;
while (!infile.eof())
{
            sum += num;
            count++;
            infile >> num;
}
```

6. In the code segment above, `infile` extracts the next value from the file before testing for the end of file at the beginning of the loop. This process is called which of the following?

    a. Short circuiting

    b. Casting

    c. Priming

    d. Recursing

    e. Overloading

7. With reference to the code segment above, another way to support the looping process might be which of the following?

    a. `while( infile.eof() != false)`

    b. `while( infile += num)`

    c. `while( infile.eof() >> true)`

    d. `while( infile >> num)`

    e. `while(!infile.eof() != true)`

8. Use the following code segment:

```
    apstring mystring;
    ifstream infile;
getstring(infile, mystring);
```

Which one of the following would be the correct prototype for the function `getstring`?

    a. `ifstream &getstring(const ofstream &I, apstring &s);`

    b. `void getstring(ifstream &I, apstring &s);`

    c. `ifstream getstring(const ifstream &I, const apstring &s);`

    d. `void getstring(const ofstream &I, const apstring &s);`

MATCHING

Place the letter of the keystroke on the right that will execute the highlight movement on the left.

_____ **1.** A holding place for data	**a.**	stream
_____ **2.** The type of stream used to receive input stream from a file	**b.**	input file
_____ **3.** Sending or receiving data elements one at a time	**c.**	extraction operator
_____ **4.** The type of stream used to send output data to a file	**d.**	source device
_____ **5.** A conduit that passes information from a sender to a receiver	**e.**	insertion operator
_____ **6.** To search items starting with the first data item	**f.**	buffer
_____ **7.** An example of this is the keyboard because data are received from the keyboard via an input stream	**g.**	destination device
_____ **8.** Used to send data to the terminal screen or output file	**h.**	serial processing
_____ **9.** Used to receive data from the keyboard or input file	**i.**	output file stream
_____ **10.** An example of this is a monitor because data are sent to the screen via an output stream	**j.**	sequential search

WRITTEN QUESTIONS

Write your answers to the following questions.
Use the program provided below to answer questions 1–4.

```cpp
// Program file: file.cpp

// This program saves your input numbers to a file, and
// then reads them from the file and displays them on the screen.

#include <iostream.h>
#include <fstream.h>

int main()
{
    ofstream outfile;
    ifstream infile;
    int upper, whole_number;

    outfile.open("numbers");
    cout << "Enter the number of numbers to be output: ";
    cin >> upper;
    for(int i = 1; i<= upper; ++i)
        outfile << i << endl;

    outfile.close();

    infile.open("numbers");
    infile >> whole_number;
    while(!infile.eof() || ! infile.fail())
    {
        cout << whole_number << endl;
        infile >> whole_number;
    }
    infile.close();
    return 0;
}
```

1. Compile and run the program. Test it with the input numbers 1, 10, and 0. What are the outputs for each run?

_____

_____

_____

2. Insert a statement to output the value of `whole_number` at the bottom of the loop (instead of the top) and test the program with the number 10 as input. Explain the result.

_____

_____

_____

_____

_____

_____

_____

_____

_____

_____

_____

_____

3. Explain why a priming input operation is performed before the end-of-file condition is tested in the program.

_____

_____

_____

_____

_____

_____

_____

4. Modify the program to perform input and output of strings. Include the apstring library, change the data type of `whole_number` to apstring, and prompt the user for the `value of string1` on each pass through the for loop. Explain any changes in output that occur when compared with the previous runs of the program.

_____

_____

_____

_____

5. Explain what the following function does:

```
ofstream outfile;

outfile.open("myfile");
outfile << 23 << endl;
outfile << "Hi there!" << endl;
outfile << 3.1416 << endl;
outfile.close();
```

_____

_____

_____

_____

6. Explain what the following function does:

```
ifstream infile;
int num;
apstring string1;
double realNum;

infile.open("myfile");
infile >> num >>string1 >> realNum;
infile.close();
```

_____

_____

_____

7. Explain what the following function does:

```
apstring filename;
cout << "Enter the input file name: ";
cin >> filename;

if (filename.length() <= 12)
    infile.open(filename.c_str());
else
   cout << "File name must not exceed 12 characters. " << endl;
```

_____

_____

_____

_____

8. Explain what the following program will do when executed:

```cpp
#include <iostream.h>
#include <fstream.h>

int main()
{
 int count = 0;
 ifstream infile;
 ofstream outfile;
 char ch;

 infile.open("myfile");
 outfile.open("copy");

 infile.get(ch);
 while (!infile.eof() && ! infile.fail())
 {
  if (ch == '\n')
  ++count;
  outfile.put(ch);
  infile.get(ch);
 }

 infile.close();
 outfile.close();
 cout << "There are " << count << " lines in the file." << endl;
 return 0;
}
```

_____

_____

_____

_____

_____

9. What are the five abstract operations that stream processing requires?

_____

_____

_____

_____

_____

10. When refering to ouput stream, explain what is meant by abstract and portable.

_____

_____

_____

_____

_____

_____

_____

_____

_____

_____

_____

_____

11. Describe what happens if you open a file for output that already exists.

_____

12. Give an example of a situation that may require that more than one file be opened at a time.

_____

_____

IN THE LAB

PROJECT 7-1

Design, implement, and test a function that counts and displays the number of words in a file.

PROJECT 7-2

Design, implement, and test a function that displays the longest word in a file.

PROJECT 7-3

Design, implement, and test a function that displays the average length of a word in a file.

PROJECT 7-4

Design, implement, and test a function that removes every instance of a user's input letter from a file.

PROJECT 7-5

The Third Interdenominational Church has on file a list of all of its benefactors (a maximum of 20 names, each up to 30 characters) along with the number of donations given and the amount of each donation that each has donated to the church. For example, the file could look like the following:

Seemann   5
12.00
15.00
35.00
20.00
18.00

Calkins   3
18.00
10.00
5.00

Shane   2
75.00
15.00

You have been asked to write a program that does the following:

Print the name of each donor and the total amount of donations given by each.
Print the total amount of donations given.
Print the largest single amount donated and the name of the benefactor who made this donation.
The program should print this information to a separate file. The output file could look like the following:

Seemann $100.00
Calkins $ 33.00
Shane $ 90.00
Grand Total: $220.00
Largest single amount donation: Shane $75.00

PROJECT 7-6

The data file `Proj7_6.txt` contains a list of instructors in your school along with the room number to which each is assigned. Write a program that, given the name of the instructor, does a linear search to find and print the room to which the instructor is assigned.

LESSON 8   VECTORS AND MATRICES

FILL IN THE BLANK

Complete the following sentences by writing the word or words in the blanks provided.

1. A(n) _____ must be used to reference a specific data item in a vector.

2. A(n) _____ is a two-dimensional array.

3. The most common searching algorithm is called a(n) _____.

4. A(n) _____ is a one-dimensional array.

5. The _____ of an array refers to the number of data items actually available in a data structure.

6. A memory location of a particular data item in a vector or matrix is called a(n) _____.

7. A data structure that can represent a list of data is called a(n) _____.

8. Vectors that have the same length and whose data are related to each other are called _____.

9. The sorting technique that is least efficient for a list of items that is almost in order is the _____.

10. The sorting technique that is similar to the way in which someone would sort a poker hand is called a(n) _____.

TRUE/FALSE

Circle T if the statement is true or F if the statement is false.

T   F   1. Once a vector is declared, elements can be accessed individually to change their value.

T   F   2. A vector can have as many variable types as necessary.

T   F   3. A list of variables accessed using a single identifier is called a vector.

T   F   4. Each of the items within a vector is referred to as an element.

T   F   5. The physical size of a vector is specified when the vector is declared.

T   F   6. A vector can be declared without specifying the data type for the variables it will contain.

T   F   7. If a vector is declared with five elements, the elements are indexed from one to five.

T   F   8. The length function returns an integer value which is the length of the vector.

MULTIPLE CHOICE

Select the best response for the following statements.

1. The number contained in brackets that determines which element of a vector is to be accessed is called the _____.

    a. superscript
    b. index
    c. vector
    d. identifier

2. Which of the following statements could be used to assign the contents of one vector to another?
   a. `vect2[all] = vect1[all];`
   b. `copy vect2 -> vect1;`
   c. `vect2 = vect1;`
   d. None of the above.

Use the following code to answer Questions 3 and 4:

```
void someFunction()
{
    const char sp = ' ';
    apvector <int> charCounter;
    apstring sentence("Once upon a time!");
    int index = 0;
    char testChar;

    while (sentence[index] != '!')
    {
        if (testChar != sp)
        {
            testChar = tolower(sentence[index]);
    charIndex = char(testChar - 'a');
    charCounter[charIndex]++;
    }
            index++;

    }
}
```

3. Running or attempting to run this program causes which of the following?
   a. The value at `charCounter[0]` is 4.
   b. The value at `charCounter[1]` is 4.
   c. The program will not build or link correctly.
   d. The program aborts due to an assertion failure.
   e. The program will cause a run-time error due to an infinite loop.

4. For purposes of accurate letter-frequency counting in this function, which of the following would be the best approach to initializing the `charCounter` elements to 0?
   a. `apvector <0> charCounter;`
   b. `apvector <int> charCounter(0);`
   c. `apvector <int> charCounter(0,26);`
   d. `apvector <int> charCounter (26,0);`
   e. The initialization to zero is automatic; no further code required.

5. If you want to make a vector of names so that the vector can hold 150 single names, which of the following is the correct format?
   a. `apstring names(50);`
      `apvector<names> List(150);`
   b. `apstring names;`
      `apvector <names> List(150);`
   c. `apvector <apstring> List (150);`

```
    d. apstring <apvector> List(150);
    e. apvector<apstring> List;
```

MATCHING

Place the letter of the keystroke on the right that will execute the highlight movement on the left.

_____ **1.** A one-dimensional array of data

_____ **2.** The most common searching algorithm. The first item is examined and each subsequent data item is examined until a match is found or the end of the vector is reached

_____ **3.** A sorting algorithm in which the smallest data item is exchanged with another item until all data are in order

_____ **4.** A data structure that can represent a list of data

_____ **5.** A sorting algorithm in which items that are directly next to each other are compared and swapped until all items are in order

_____ **6.** A memory location of a particular data item in a vector or matrix

_____ **7.** An error that occurs when an index value less than 0 or greater than the size of the array is used

_____ **8.** The available memory units for storing data items in a data structure

_____ **9.** A two dimensional array of data

_____ **10.** The relative position of the components of an array

_____ **11.** The number of data items actually available in a data structure at a specific time

_____ **12.** A sorting algorithm that works much like the sorting through a hand of cards. One item is compared to all the items and inserted in the proper place

_____ **13.** Vectors that have the same length and whose data are related to each other

a. array

b. vector

c. sequential search

d. index

e. bubble sort

f. selection sort

g. parallel vectors

h. cell

i. physical size

j. insertion sort

k. range bound error

l. logical size

m. matrix

WRITTEN QUESTIONS

Write your answers to the following questions.

1. Next to each line of the following code, write an explanation for what the outcome of that line is.

```
apvector<int> list1(10), list2(20,6);      _____
                                           _____
apvector <double> list3;                   _____
                                           _____
cout << "Length of list1 = " <<list1.length() << endl;  _____
                                           _____
for(i = 0; i < list2.length(); i++)
    cout << list2[i] << endl;              _____
                                           _____
list1 = list2;                             _____
```

```
list3.resize(40);                              _____
                                               _____
cout << list3[0] << endl;                      _____
                                               _____
cout << list1[40] << endl;                     _____
                                               _____
                                               _____
```

2. Next to each line of the following code, write an explanation for what the outcome of that line is.

```
apmatrix <int> m1(10,10), m2(20,20,6);         _____

                                               _____

apmatrix <double> m3;                          _____

                                               _____

cout << "m1 has " << m1.numrows()
     << " rows and " << m1.numcols()
     << " columns." << endl;                   _____

                                               _____
for(row = 0; row < m2.numrows(); row++)
    for (col = 0; col < m2.numcols(); col++)
        cout << m2[row][col] << endl;
    cout << endl;
}

m1 = m2;                                        _____
                                               _____
list3.resize(20,10);                           _____
                                               _____
cout << m3[0] << endl;                          _____

cout << m3[40] << endl;                         _____
                                               _____
```

Use the following code to answer questions 3–7.

```
// Program file: vecdrive.cpp
//
// This program invokes vector processing functions to
//
// 1. Read integers into a vector from the keyboard
// 2. Display the contents of the vector to the screen
// 3. Sort the vector contents in ascending order
// 4. Display the contents of the sorted vector

#include <iostream.h>
#include "apvector.h"
```

```
void sort(apvector<int> &v);

int findmin( apvector <int> &v, int first);

void swap(int &x, int &y);

void printvector(apvector<int> &v);

int main()
{
apvector <int> number(10);
int numbers;

cout << "How many numbers will you be entering?";
cin >> l;
number.resize(l);
for(int i = 0; i < number.length(); i++)
  {
   cout << "Please enter a number: ";
   cin >> number[i];
}

cout << "The contents in your vector are: ";
printvector(number);

cout << endl;

cout << "The sorted version of your vector is: ";
sort(number);
printvector(number);

return 0;
}


void printvector(apvector<int> &v)
{
for(int j = 0; j<v.length(); j++)
  cout << v[j] << " ";
}


void sort(apvector<int> &v)
{
int min = 0;
    for (int k = 0; k < v.length() - 1; k++)
{
```

```
        min = findmin(v, k);
        if(min != k)
                          swap(v[k], v[min]);
    }
}


    int findmin( apvector <int> &v, int first)
    {
     int minI = first;

     for(int x = first + 1; x < v.length(); x++)
        if (v[x] < v[minI])
                          minI = x;
        return minI;
    }

    void swap(int &x, int &y)
    {
     int temp = x;
     x = y;
     y = temp;
    }
```

3. Enter, compile, and run the program. Test it with data sets of varying sizes (sizes 0, 1, and 10). What are the outputs for each run?

_____

_____

_____

_____

4. Experiment with this code to see what happens when a vector index is out of range. For example, change the middle parameter in the for loops to adjust the number of times the loop is run through. Explain what happens.

_____

5. Take out the resize line in the main section of the program and run it. Explain what happens.

_____

_____

_____

6. What type of sort is being used in this program?

_____

7. How could the sort function be written to sort in descending rather that ascending order?

_____

_____

8. Write a statement that declares a vector of type `apstring` with 10 elements in it called names.

_____

9. Give an example of a situation where a vector could be used in a program.

_____

10. Write a loop that will print the values in a vector named **grades** to the screen.

_____

_____

11. Declare and initialize a two-dimensional array or matrix that could store the data below:

       1.223   6.482   3.987

       4.008   3.572   1.982

_____

12. Write code that will fill the two-dimensional array declared above with the values given in number 11.

_____

_____

_____

_____

_____

_____

13. Write code that would allow the user to enter the values in number 11 into the declared variable **values**.

_____

_____

_____

_____

_____

_____

_____

_____

IN THE LAB
PROJECT 8-1

Write a program that asks the user for his or her name and stores it in string. The program should then print the user's name to the screen by dividing the characters between the lines and presenting them diagonally as in the example below:

```
J
   e
      r
      r
         y


         G
            a
               r
                  c
                     i
                        a
```

PROJECT 8-2

Write a program that declares a two-dimensional array (matrix) of integers with four rows and four columns and uses a loop to initialize the vector in the pattern below. *Hint:* Figure out a pattern of the numbers in the vector to discover a simple way to initialize the matrix.

0	0	0	0
0	1	2	3
0	2	4	6
0	3	6	9

PROJECT 8-3

Write a function called `multMat` that accepts two integer `apmatrix` quantities, multiplies them together, and returns the results to a third variable. The function definition is as follows:

```
void multMat( apmatrix &A, apmatrix &B, apmatrix &prod)
// This function takes two two-dimensional arrays and multiplies them together
// The sizes of the two matrices must be the same
// Input: Two integer matricies
// Output: The product of the two matrices
```

PROJECT 8-4

Write a function subtract() that will calculate the differences between each of the items in an apvector quantity and the given mean. The function definition is as follows:

```
void subtract( apvector<double> &n, double mean)
// This function will find the difference between each element of a vector and
the given mean.
//
// Input: The vector and the mean.
// Output: The vector will now hold values for the difference of the old value
and the mean.
```

PROJECT 8-5

The following table shows the total sales for salespeople of the Falcon Manufacturing Company:

Salesperson	Week 1	Week 2	Week 3
Kym Sopha	30	25	45
Matt McCallum	22	32	35
Kimberly Clark	12	19	25
Alisha Lake	32	33	31
Hannah McGee	22	17	28

The price of the product being sold is $3250.25. Write a program that permits input of the data in the table and displays both a replica of the table and a table showing the dollar value of sales for each individual during each week along with their total sales. Also, print the total sales for each week and the total sales for the company over the three week period.

LESSON 9   INTRODUCTION TO USER-DEFINED CLASSES

FILL IN THE BLANKS

Complete the following sentences by writing the word or words in the blanks provided.

1. Using a built-in operator (like +, =, etc.) to designate an operation on a new data type is called _____.

2. The operator that returns an object to which a pointer is pointing is denoted with the symbol: * and is called the _____.

3. A particular instance of a class is called a(n) _____.

4. A building model of a real world object is called a(n) _____.

5. _____ are functions that belong to a class.

TRUE/FALSE

Circle T if the statement is true or F if the statement is false.

T F 1. Classes can only be used for one driver program.

T F 2. Procedural programming is the same as object-oriented programming.

T F 3. Constructor functions are used to declare variables of a specific data type.

T F 4. A class in C++ consists of a declaration section and an implementation section.

T F 5. Private member functions cannot be accessed or called on in any way.

T F 6. It is not possible to overload the operator = in C++.

T F 7. Many of the operators in C++ are polymorphic.

T F 8. One of the most serious problems posed by large software systems is that of maintaining them over a period of years.

MULTIPLE CHOICE

Select the best response for the following statements.

Use the following code for questions 1 – 4. (Note that enumerations are discussed in Appendix F of text.)

```
#ifndef TIME_CLASS_H
#define TIME_CLASS_H

#include "apstring.h"

enum DayNite {AM, PM };

class TimeClass
{
public:
    TimeClass();
    TimeClass( const TimeClass &);
    TimeClas ( int, int, int, DayNite );
```

```
        void SetHour(int);
        void SetMinute(int);
        void SetSecond(int);
        void Setampm(DayNite);

        int GetHour() const;
        int GetMinute() const;
        int GetSecond() const;
        DayNite {AM, PM} const;
        apstring ReturnTimeString();

        TimeClass operator + (const TimeClass &);
        TimeClass &operator = (const TimeClass &);

    private:
        int hours;
        int minutes;
        int seconds;
        DayNite DN;
    }
    #endif
```

1. Having declared the class above, the class members will have to be defined. What will the names of the files for declaring and defining most likely be?
   a. The class declaration and definitions(s) will be in "timeclass.h".
   b. The class declaration and definitions(s) will be in "timeclass.cpp".
   c. Only the class declaration shown above will be in "timeclass.h".
   d. Only the class definition(s) will be in "timeclass.h".
   e. Only the class declaration shown above will be in "timeclass.cpp".

2. Using `#ifndef` and `#define` in the above code segment will result in which of the following?
   a. The linker will only process this source code once.
   b. The builder will only process this source code once.
   c. The compiler will only process this source code once.
   d. The interpreter will only process this source code once.
   e. The executable file will only process this source code once.

3. Given the code segment above, which of the following would **not** be a correct implementation of the class constructors?
   a. `TimeClass::TimeClass()`
   ```
      {
      {
   ```
   b. `TimeClass::TimeClass()`
   ```
      {
          hours = 0;
          minutes = 0;
          seconds = 0;
          DN = AM;
      }
   ```

```
c. TimeClass::TimeClass( const TimeClass &incoming)
   {
       incoming = *this;
   }
```

```
d. TimeClass::TimeClass( int Hr, int Mi, int Se, DayNite dn)
   : hours(Hr), minutes(Mi), seconds(Se), DN(dn) { }
```

```
e. TimeClass::TimeClass(int Hr, int Mi, int Se, DayNite dn)
   {
       hours = Hr;
       minutes = Mi;
       seconds = Se;
       DN = dn;
   }
```

4. Which of the following might be appropriate for setting the hour value for an object of `TimeClass`?

  I.
```
TimeClass TimeObject;
TimeObject.hour = 8;
```
  II.
```
TimeClass TimeObject;
TimeObject = 8;
```
  III.
```
TimeClass TimeObject;
TimeObject.SetHour(8);
```

  a. I only

  b. II only

  c. III only

  d. I and III only

  e. I and II only

5. Functions and variables declared in a class definition are called

  a. members.

  b. objects.

  c. instances.

  d. methods.

  e. procedures.

6. Deriving one object from an already existing object is called

  a. derivation.

  b. construction.

  c. inheritance.

  d. dereference.

  e. containment.

7. A particular instance of a class is called a(n)

  a. member.

  b. function.

  c. data abstraction.

  d. object.

  e. None of the above.

MATCHING

Place the letter of the keystroke on the right that will execute the highlight movement on the left.

_____ 1. A particular instance of a class	**a.** data structure
_____ 2. Using a built-in operator to designate an operation	**b.** accessor
_____ 3. Members of a function that can be referenced by any module that includes the class library	**c.** copy constructor
	d. data member
_____ 4. The event of designating the operators to the same general operations (+, =, etc.) even though the actual operations performed may be different depending on the data type being used	**e.** encapsulation
	f. modifier
_____ 5. A way of organizing data items so that they can be treated as a unit	**g.** polymorphism
	h. private member
_____ 6. Data types that provide operations for a set of functions used on a data structure	**i.** object
	j. abstract data type
_____ 7. Member functions that return the value of attributes	**k.** class
_____ 8. A building model of a real world object	**l.** data abstraction
_____ 9. A function that is run when an object of the ADT is passed by value as a parameter to a function	**m.** default
_____ 10. The process of separating functions and associating a set of functions with particular data structures	**n.** formal specifications
	o. member function
_____ 11. This occurs when the user of a data type is not able to access the components parts of an ADT except by invoking the operations	**p.** public member
	q. operator overloading

_____ 12. Encapsulted member functions that cannot be referenced directly by programmers who are using the class

_____ 13. After user requirements are written this description of constructor inputs, outputs, and any other assumptions about their data or the effects of an operation is written

_____ 14. The functions that belong to a class

_____ 15. The data belonging to a class

_____ 16. The constructor used if no other specifications are given when a variable of the ADT is declared

_____ 17. Member functions that modify the values of attributes

WRITTEN QUESTIONS

Write your answers to the following questions.

1. What are some reasons you may need to use the point ADT?

   _____

   _____

   _____

   _____

2. Give some examples of ADTs we've already used in this course.

   _____

   _____

3. How could you use the point ADT to search a matrix for the number 47?

   _____

   _____

   _____

   _____

   _____

   _____

   _____

   _____

   _____

4. Why might you want to use the set class?

   _____

   _____

5. What information is associated with a student in the student class?

   _____

   _____

6. How could you use the student class to get the average for a student who has test scores of 82, 78, and 97?

   _____

   _____

   _____

   _____

   _____

_____

_____

7. What is the purpose of an abstract data type?

_____

_____

8. In what ways can a student be declared in a program using the student class?

_____

_____

_____

_____

9. What are the two parts of the description part of an individual class in C++?

_____

_____

_____

_____

10. What is the purpose of using a constructor in a class?

_____

_____

_____

_____

11. What does the reserved word `this` do?

_____

_____

12. What does the `toString` operator do?

_____

_____

_____

For questions 13 and 15, use the following class declarations:

```
class DateClass
{
public:
```

```
    DateClass();
    DateClass(int yr, int mo, int dt, int da);
    // Sets the date with the following quantities:
    // -year (yr) given as an integer
    // - month (mo) given as an integer
    // - date (dt) given as an integer
    // - day (da) given as an integer

    void SetDate(int yr, int mo, int dt, int da);
    // sets the date as specified above

    void GetDate(int &yr, int &mo, int &dt, int &da);
    // returns the date integers as specified above

    void incrementDate();

private:
  bool isLeap();
     // precondition:  year is initialized, such that year >= 0
     // postcondition: function returns true if the member value
     // is a leap year, otherwise false is returned

  int GetDaysInMonth();
  // precondition:  the month value is initialized, such that 1 <= month <= 12
  // postcondition:  the function returns the number of days for the month member
  // value, and the year member value.  For example,
  // GetDaysInMonth(4, 1998) returns 30

  void IncrementDay();
  // precondition:  the member value day is initialized such that it is
  // between 1 and 7, inclusively.
  // postcondition: the member value day is one more than it was, or 1
  // if the day is incremented past 7

  void IncrementMonth();
  // precondition:  the member value month is initialized such that it is
  // between 1 and 12, inclusively.
  // postcondition: the member value month is one more than it was, or
  // 1 if the month value is incremented past 12

  int year; // holds the value of the year as an integer
  int month; // holds the value of the month as an integer
  int date; // holds the value of the date of the month as an integer
  int day;  // holds the value of the day (1 = sunday, 2 = monday, etc) as
     // an integer
  };
```

13. Write the implementation for the member function `IncrementDay()`, given the above header and conditions.

_____

_____

_____

_____

_____

_____

_____

_____

14. Write the implementation for the member function `IncrementMonth()`, given the above header and conditions.

_____

_____

_____

_____

_____

_____

_____

15. Write the member function `IncrementDate()`, given the following header and conditions. Use the member function `GetDaysInMonth()`, as specified in the class declaration above, and the `IncrementDay()` and `IncrementMonth()` as specified above and written in questions 13 and 14.

```
void DateClass::IncrementDate()
// precondition:  member values year, month, and date are initialized such that
//        year >= 0, month is between 1 and 12, and date is between 1 and the
maximum date in the given month
// postcondition:   the day member is incremented by one, which includes
incrementing the month member //value and the year member value as appropriate.
```

_____

_____

_____

_____

_____

_____

_____

_____

_____

_____

_____

The following is a random generator class and a tester program. Key the header file in as a header file, the implementation file as an implementation of the header, and finally the test file. After testing the program, answer questions 16 and 17.

```cpp
// Class declaration file (header file): random.h
//
// Objects of this class generate random numbers
// between specified lower and upper bounds.

#ifndef RANDOM_H

class randomGen
{

public:
 // Class constructor
 randomGen();

 // Member function

 int nextNum(int low, int high);
};
#define RANDOM_H
#endif



// Class implementation file: random.cpp
#include <stdlib.h>
#include <time.h>
#include "random.h"

randomGen::randomGen()
{
 time_t seconds;
 time(& seconds);
 srand((unsigned int) seconds);
}
```

```cpp
int randomGen:: nextNum(int low, int high)
{
 return rand() % (high - low + 1) + low;
}



// Program file: randdriv.cpp
// Tests the distribution of random numbers between 1 and 6 for a user-specified
number of tries.

#include <iostream.h>
#include <iomanip.h>
#include "random.h"
#include "apvector.h"


const int MAX_NUM = 6;

int main()
{
 randomGen myGen;
 apvector<int> stats;
 stats.resize(MAX_NUM);
 int num_tries = 0, number = 0;

 // Initialize vector of statistics
 for (int i = 0; i < MAX_NUM; i++)
    stats[i] = 0;

 // Obtain number of tries
 cout << "Enter the number of tries: ";
 cin >> num_tries;

 // Obtain random statistics
 for (int j = 1; j <= num_tries; j++)
 {
    number = myGen.nextNum(1,MAX_NUM);
    stats[number - 1] = stats[number - 1] + 1;
 }

 // Display statistics
 cout << "Number Frequency" << endl << endl;

 for(int x = 0; x < MAX_NUM; x++)
    cout << x+ 1 << " " << setw(5) << stats[x] << endl;
 return 0;
}
```

16. Compile and run the random number driver program. Record the results of three runs of the program in the following table:

Random Number	Frequency (6 tries)	Frequency (60 tries)	Frequency (600 tries)
1			
2			
3			
4			
5			
6			

Does the distribution of tries improve as the number of tries increases? _____

17. Modify the random driver program so that it generates numbers from 1 to 10. Then fill in the following table with your test results:

Random Number	Frequency (10 tries)	Frequency (100 tries)	Frequency (1000 tries)
1			
2			
3			
4			
5			
6			
7			
8			
9			
10			

Comparing the two tables, what happens to the distribution of tries when the range of numbers is increased?

_____

_____

_____

_____

IN THE LAB

PROJECT 9-1

Write a class called circle. This class should allow programmers to find the area and circumference **of a** circle. After you've written a class, write a test driver that tests the class.

PROJECT 9-2

Write a program to be used by the registrar of a university. The program should get information from the **keyboard**, and the data for each student should include: student name; student number; classification (1 for **freshman**, 2 for sophomore, 3 for junior, 4 for senior, or 7 for special student); hours completed; hours taken; **and grade**-point average. You should design a class to represent a student as an abstract data type.

LESSON 10   CLASS TEMPLATES, POLYMORPHISM, AND INHERITANCE

FILL IN THE BLANKS

Complete the following sentences by writing the word or words in the blanks provided.

1. A class that other classes may inherit attributes and behavior from is a(n) _____.

2. In a class declaration of a derived class, the access specifier follows a(n) _____ mark.

3. Redefining an operation that already has meaning, such as the plus sign (+), is one example of _____.

4. Protected members of a class behave like _____ for derived classes, but like _____ for any other classes in a system.

5. When an integer is added to a real number, the addition operation promotes the integer operand to a real number first, adds it to the real number, and finally returns a real number result. In this case, the addition operation is known as a(n) _____.

TRUE/FALSE

Circle T if the statement is true or F if the statement is false.

T F 1. C++ is the only programming language that supports polymorphism.

T F 2. It is acceptable for one class to use the functions of another class.

T F 3. The term "protected member" means the same thing as "private member".

T F 4. In C++ users can specify the element types contained in objects.

T F 5. C++ operators can be overloaded by defining them as free functions.

T F 6. The notation in a class implementation file for a class template is different than the notation used in an ordinary class implementation file.

MULTIPLE CHOICE

Select the best response for the following statements.
Use the following code segment for question 1:

```
TimeClass &operator = (const TimeClass &inComing)
{
  hours = inComing.GetHour();
  minutes = inComing.GetMinute();
  seconds = incoming.GetSeconds();
  DN = inComing.GetAmPm();
  return *this;
}
```

1. Given the header code of the above operator function, which of the following would **not** be allowed inside the operator = function definition?
   a. hour = hour + 12;
   b. newString = inComing.ReturnTimeString();
   c. tempHour(inComing);

    d. `inComing.SetHour(12);`

    e. All of the above would be allowed.

2. Another way to describe containment is
    a. inheritance.
    b. reusability.
    c. has-a relation.
    d. is-a relation.
    e. None of the above.

3. If the programmer of a class wants to make it possible for a user to specify the item type to be used in the class when the object is created, the programmer should use a
    a. polymorphism.
    b. class declaration.
    c. public member function.
    d. class template.
    e. None of the above.

4. Which of the following are NOT different in the class implementation file for a class template and that of an ordinary class implementation file?
    a. The compiler directive `# include <ctemp.h>` must be used.
    b. Notation.
    c. Class declaration file does not have to be included.
    d. All of the above are differences.
    e. None of the above are necessary.

5. If a class inherits common abstract data and behavior from another class, it is a
    a. base class.
    b. class hierarchy.
    c. access specifier.
    d. derived class.
    e. None of the above.

IDENTIFY IS-A / HAS-A RULE

Write "is a" or "has a" to indicate the relationship between the objects on the blank line between each column. Example:

    A bike   <u>has a</u>   wheel

1. A forest   ————   tree

2. A school   ————   building

3. A dog   ————   animal

4. A song   ————   beat

5. A calculator   ————   display window

6. A book   ————   cover

7. A ball   ————   sphere

8. A keyboard _____ key

9. A telephone _____ form of communication

10. A car _____ steering wheel

MATCHING

Place the letter of the keystroke on the right that will execute the highlight movement on the left.

_____ 1. A data or function member of a class that is visible to a derived class but not to any other part of the program

_____ 2. The use of one operator to denote many different operations

_____ 3. Describes the relationship between two classes when one class has another class contained within it

_____ 4. The reuse of attributes and behavior of other classes in a heirarchy

_____ 5. Describes the relationship between two classes that are related by inheritance

_____ 6. A class that allows the user to specify the data types when the class is called on

_____ 7. A type of function that allows the specified type variable name to be treated as a formal type parameter

_____ 8. Non-member functions used to manipulate class data types

_____ 9. A class that is obtained partly by inheriting all of the common, more abstract data and behavior of another class

_____ 10. Another name for the has-a relation

_____ 11. Allows users to specify item type when objects are related

_____ 12. A way of relating classes to each other

_____ 13. A class that other classes may inherit attributes and behavior from

_____ 14. The word ("public" or "private") that follows a single colon after the name of a derived class is given in the declaration

a.   access specifier

b.   class heirarchy

c.   containment

d.   free function

e.   has-a relation

f.   is-a relation

g.   protected member

h.   polymorphism

i.   inheritance

j.   generic class

k.   function template

l.   derived class

m.   class template

n.   base class

WRITTEN QUESTIONS

Write your answers to the following questions.

1. What is the relationship between a base class and a derived class?

_____

2. What is one advantage of using class templates?

_____

3. What are the components of a class template?

_____

_____

4. What are the differences between a class implementation file for a class template and an ordinary class implementation file?

_____

_____

_____

_____

5. Why might someone want to use the rational class developed in this lesson?

_____

_____

6. Why did the <<, >>, +, *, =, == operators have to be defined and implemented in the rational class? That is, why couldn't the user just rely on the pre-existing definitions?

_____

_____

7. What is the output for this code (assuming the use of the rational class developed and implemented in this lesson)?

```
Rational twoFifths(2,5);
cout << setiosflags(ios::fixed | ios::showpoint);
cout << twoFifths + 1 << endl;
cout << twoFifths + .5 << endl;
```

_____

_____

_____

8. What are two ways in which classes can be reused in object-oriented programming?

_____

_____

_____

9. How does a computer decide where to find the implementation of data or member functions (in a base or derived class)?

_____

_____

Use the following code to answer questions 10 – 12:

```
///////////////////////////////////////////////////
Class declaration file: rational.h
#ifndef RATIONAL_H
#define RATIONAL_H
#include <iostream.h>

class rational
{
 public:

 // Constructors

 rational();
 rational (int numerator, int denominator);
 rational (const rational &r);

 // Accesors
 int numerator() const;
 int denominator() const;

 // Assignment
 const rational& operator = (const rational &rhs);

 private:
 // Data members
 int my_numerator, my_denominator;

 //Utility function
 //void reduce();

};

// The following free (non-member) functions operate on rational numbers

// Arithmetic
rational operator + (const rational &lhs, const rational &rhs);

rational operator - (const rational &lhs, const rational &rhs);

rational operator * (const rational &lhs, const rational &rhs);

rational operator / (const rational &lhs, const rational &rhs);
```

```cpp
// Comparison
bool operator == (const rational &lhs, const rational &rhs);

// Input and output
istream & operator >> (istream &is, rational &r);
ostream& operator << (ostream &os, const rational &r);


#endif

/////////////////////////////////////////////////////////
Implementation file for rational class

#include <assert.h>

#include "rational.h"


rational::rational()
{
 my_numerator = 1;
 my_denominator = 1;
}

rational::rational(int numerator, int denominator)
{
 assert(denominator != 0);
 my_numerator = numerator;
 my_denominator = denominator;

}

rational::rational(const rational &r)
{
 my_numerator = r.my_numerator;
 my_denominator = r.my_denominator;
}

const rational& rational::operator = (const rational &rhs)
{
 my_numerator = rhs.numerator();
 my_denominator = rhs.denominator();
 return *this;
}
```

```
int rational::numerator() const
{
 return my_numerator;
}

int rational::denominator() const
{
 return my_denominator;
}

rational operator + (const rational &lhs,
 const rational &rhs)
{
 int numerator = lhs.numerator() * rhs. denominator()
  + rhs. numerator() * lhs.denominator();
 int denominator = lhs.denominator() * rhs.denominator();
 rational sum(numerator, denominator);
 return sum;
}

rational operator - (const rational &lhs,
 const rational &rhs)
{
 you will be asked to write this code in the questions below
}

rational operator * (const rational &lhs,
 const rational &rhs)
{
 int numerator = lhs.numerator() * rhs.numerator();
 int denominator = lhs.denominator() * rhs.denominator();
 rational product(numerator, denominator);
 return product;
}

rational operator / (const rational &lhs,
 const rational &rhs)
{
YOU WILL BE ASKED TO WRITE THIS CODE IN THE QUESTIONS BELOW
}

bool operator == (const rational &lhs, const rational &rhs)
{
 return  (lhs.numerator()  ==  rhs.numerator())  &&  (lhs.denominator()  ==
rhs.denominator());
}
```

```
ostream& operator << (ostream &os, const rational &r)
{
 os << r.numerator() << "/" << r.denominator();
 return os;
}

istream& operator >> (istream &is, rational &r)
{
 char division_symbol;
 int numerator = 0, denominator = 0;

 is >> numerator >> division_symbol >> denominator;
 assert(division_symbol == '/');
 assert(denominator != 0);
 rational number(numerator, denominator);
 r = number;
 return is;
}


//////////////////////////////////////////////////////////
Program file: ratdriv.cpp

#include <iostream.h>
#include "rational.h"

int main()
{
 rational r1, r2, r3, r4;

 cout << "Enter the first number (<integer>/<integer>): ";
 cin >> r1;
 cout << "Enter the second number (<integer>/<integer>): ";
 cin >> r2;
 cout << "Enter the third number (<integer>/<integer>): ";
 cin >> r3;

 cout << "The result of r1 + r2 * r3 is:" << r1 + r2 *r3 << endl;



 return 0;
}
```

10. Compile and run the rational number driver program. Use the program to fill in the following table:

r1	r2	r3	Output
1/3	1/2	1/2	
1/2	3/4	7/8	
3/2	3/2	1/2	

11. Complete the functions for subtracting and dividing rational numbers. Then add a line to your test driver (r1 – r2 / r3) to test your functions on these values:

r1	r2	r3	Output
1/3	1/2	1/2	
1/2	3/4	7/8	
3/2	3/2	1/2	

_____

_____

_____

_____

_____

_____

_____

_____

_____

_____

_____

_____

_____

_____

_____

_____

_____

_____

12. Modify the output operation for rational numbers so that it displays just the numerator (a whole number) when the denominator is 1.

_____

_____

_____

_____

_____

_____

_____

_____

IN THE LAB

PROJECT 10-1

Numeric and textual data are often used to represent complex information. Consider the task of managing the inventory of a compact disk mail order company. We might begin by representing the information that describes each CD that the company carries. Each CD has the following attributes:

1. A five digit identification number (this is a unique integer, so an appropriate variable type could be long, for example). This value is sometimes called the key value.

2. Title (an `apstring`).

3. A recording artist (an `apstring`).

4. A list price (a real number).

5. A wholesale price (a real number).

6. The number of these CDs currently in stock (a non-negative integer value).

7. The number of disks in the package (a positive integer value).

8. The type of music to which the recording belongs (classical, jazz, rock, country, or easy listening).

These attributes can be modeled as the data members of a new class called CD. Users of the CD class should be able to:

1. Create a new CD object with default values for each attribute.

2. Create a new CD object with user-specified attributes.

3. Observe any of the attributes of a CD.

4. Modify any of the attributes of a CD.

5. Assign the contents of one CD object to another.

6. Compare two CD objects for equality. Two CDs are the same if their identification numbers are the same.

7. Write a class declaration and implementation modules that capture the attributes and behavior of CDs as described above.

8. Write a driver module and test each member function that you have written.

9. Write a third module (consisting of header and implementation files) that defines a set of functions (not member functions of the CD class) for handling interactive input and output operations on CD objects. You should define four functions:

   a. A `display_cd` function that takes a CD object as a value parameter and displays its data members on the screen. Sample output might be the following:

ID number:	12345
Title:	Little Earthquakes
Artist:	Tori Amos
Class:	rock
List price:	15.98
Wholesale price:	11.00
Number in stock:	10
Number of disks:	1

   b. A `read_cd` function that takes a CD object as a reference parameter and prompts the user for all of the values of its attributes.

   c. A `modify_cd` function that takes a CD object as a reference parameter and displays a menu of attributes to be modified. When the user selects an attribute, the function prompts the user for the new value of the attribute, inputs this value, and stores it in the appropriate data member of the CD object.

   d. A `process_cd` function that takes a CD object as a reference parameter and displays a menu of three commands. The commands display a CD object, modify a CD object, or quit the menu. The function should invoke functions developed earlier to perform these operations, and repeat the display of the menu until the user enters the command to quit.

10. Update your driver module to test the user interface module. Begin by calling the `read_cd` function to initialize a CD object. Then pass this object to the `process_cd` function.

LESSON 11   RECURSION AND EFFICIENT SEARCHING AND SORTING

FILL IN THE BLANKS

Complete the following sentences by writing the word or words in the blanks provided.

1. A(n) _____ sort puts each element of the list into its own sublist as a first step.

2. A(n) _____ sort breaks down the original list into two partitions as a first step.

3. Simple, elegant solutions formed by recursive algorithms, such as the quick sort, are known as _____ algorithms.

4. When analyzing the space and time considerations of problems, the three behaviors that algorithms generally adhere to are _____, _____ and _____.

5. A function that calls upon itself is known as a(n) _____ function.

TRUE/FALSE

Circle T if the statement is true or F if the statement is false.

T   F   1. Recursion can be thought of as a type of looping.

T   F   2. Things that are programmed using recursion cannot be programmed using loops.

T   F   3. The factorial function can be rewritten to be a tail-recursive function.

T   F   4. Efficiency in computer programming refers to the amount of space and time required to run a program.

T   F   5. Using a combination of linear and logarithmic behavior in an algorithm is the most efficient way to write an algorithm.

T   F   6. It is preferable to write a tail-recursive function when possible.

MULTIPLE CHOICE

Select the best response for the following statements.

1. The most efficient algorithm is one that behaves in a(n) _____ manner.
   a. linear
   b. logarithmic
   c. combination logarithmic/ linear
   d. quadratic
   e. None of the above.

2. The Towers of Hanoi problem is a good example of
   a. quick sort.
   b. recursion.
   c. binary search.
   d. merge sort.
   e. stack overflow.

3. Which of the following is NOT correct with respect to the various sorting algorithms?
   a. The quicksort divides its list in equal parts as part of the process.
   b. The quicksort leaves one item sorted per action as part of the process.
   c. The quicksort requires a call to another function as part of the process.

d. The merge sort requires a call to another function as part of the process.

e. The merge sort uses a divide and conquer algorithm.

Use the following program code segment for question 4.

```
apvector<int> itemVector(numItems);
newItem = numNec;
int i = 0;
bool found = false;
while( (i < numItems ) && (!found))
{
     if (newItem == itemVector[i])
          found = true;
     i++;
}
itemVector[numItems] = newItem;
numItems++;
```

4. The process that is actually accomplished by the program code given above would best be called which one of the following?

a. Editing an item in the list.

b. Replacing an item in the list.

c. Removing an item from the list.

d. Appending an item to the end of the list.

e. Inserting an item somewhere in the middle of the list.

Consider the following program code segment for question 5.

```
apvector<apstring> NameVector(numNames);
apstring newName;

  int i= numNames — 1;
  while ((i >= 0) && (NameVector[i] > newName))
    {
        NameVector[i+1] = NameVector[i];
        i--;
    }
checkResize(numNames + 1); // added function that resizes the vector
NameVector[i] = newName;
numNames++;
```

5. Consider the following conditions related to the program code segment given above:

   - Value of newNames is Kappler

   - The local part of the NameVector list before the above code segment occurs is

       . . . Imberg, Johnson, Lerch, McChesney . . .

Assume that the above code works correctly for this question. Which one of the following would best represent the list after the above code has been executed?

a. . . . Imberg, Johnson, Johnson, Kapplar, McChesney . . .
b. . . . Imberg, Johnson, Kappler, Lerch, McChesney . . .
c. . . . Imberg, Kappler, Johnson, Lerch, McChesney . . .
d. . . . Imberg, Kappler, Lerch, Lerch, McChesney . . .
e. . . . Imberg, Imberg, Kappler, Johnson, Lerch, McChesney . . .

MATCHING

Place the letter of the keystroke on the right that will execute the highlight movement on the left.

———— **1.** A special kind of recursive function in which no work is done in the function after the recursive call

———— **2.** This occurs when the amount of stack memory available is exceeded

———— **3.** The part of memory where activation records are stored when calls to subprograms are made

———— **4.** A technique used in programming in which a function calls upon itself

———— **5.** One of the fastest sorting techniques; it uses recursion and divide and conquer strategies

———— **6.** A sorting technique that merges two sorted subvectors together

———— **7.** The distinguished item that separates a list of items in a sort

———— **8.** If a stopping state and a step leading to that stopping state are not in the design of a recursive function this type of recursion is produced

———— **9.** A complex theory of geometric forms

———— **10.** Simple and elegant solutions formed by recursive algorithms

———— **11.** An instance of a fractal shape

———— **12.** A way of dealing with data in a list such that the last data item added is the first one taken off

———— **13.** A technique for searching a sorted list in which the middle value is examined recursively to see which half contains the target value until the target is located or it is determined that the target value does not exist in the list

a. stack

b. binary search

c. divide and conquer algorithms

d. infinite recursion

e. merge sort

f. quick sort

g. c-curve

h. fractal geometry

i. pivot

j. recursion

k. run-time stack

l. tail-recursive

m. stack overflow

WRITTEN QUESTIONS

Write your answers to the following questions.

1. What are some mathematical examples of recursion?

————————————————————————————————————

————————————————————————————————————

2. What are some ways in which the efficiency of a program can be examined?

_____

_____

_____

3. Describe a linear algorithm.

_____

_____

_____

4. What are some of the benefits of recursion?

_____

_____

_____

_____

_____

5. What two assumptions have to be made in order to use a binary search?

_____

_____

6. Step through this formula and write down the output if the number of times entered as input is 3.

```cpp
#include <iostream.h>

void PrintMes(int numTimes);

int main()
{
 int n;
 cout << "How many times should the message be printed?";
 cin >> n;
 PrintMes(n);
 return 0;
}

void PrintMes(int numTimes)
{
 if(numTimes > 0)
 {
  cout << "The message" << endl;
  PrintMes(numTimes - 1);
 }
}
```

_____

_____

_____

_____

7. Write the function FindItem(), which searches through an apvector of apstring indexes called NameList, and returns the index of the apstring name that was passed to it. The function must return a value of -1 if the item is not found. Write the function using the following conditions.

```
// precondition: targetName holds the value of a name string, and NameList
//               is initialized with a list of NumNames number of names.

// postcondition: function returns the apvector index of the item if the
   name is
//                found; otherwise a -1 is returned

int FindItem(const apvector<apstring> &NameList, const apstring &targetName,
int numNames)
```

_____

_____

_____

_____

_____

_____

_____

_____

_____

_____

_____

_____

8. Write the function ShiftLeft(), which accepts an apvector of apstring names called NameList, and a lower apvector index (lowIndex) and an upper apvector index (highIndex). The function will move all items in the apvector by one to the left starting at the item at the location one more than the lower index and ending with the given upper index item. The item at the location lowIndex will be lost.

For example,

if lowIndex = 13 and highIndex = 20 then the code segment: ShiftLeft(NameList, lowIndex, highIndex);

should change the list in the following way:

original:

value --> 13 5 19 8 15 4 7 12 18 1

index --> 11 12 13 14 15 16 17 19 19 20

will change to:

value --> 13 5 8 15 4 7 12 18 1 1

index --> 11 12 13 14 15 16 17 18 19 20

Notice that the item at location 13 is lost.

Write the function `ShiftLeft()` given the conditions below:

```
// precondition: apvector NameList is initialized with n items such that n >=
  highIndex and
// 0<=lowIndex < highIndex
// postcondition: the array/vector is altered such that for every position
greater than and including lowIndex and    //less that highIndex, NameList[n]
=   NameList[n+1]. The item at NameList[lowIndex] is lost.
  void ShiftLeft(apvector<apstring> &NameList, int lowIndex, int highIndex)
```

_____

_____

_____

_____

_____

9. Write the function `DeleteItem()`, which uses `FindItem()` (from number 7) and `ShiftLeft()` (from number 8) to remove an item from an `apvector` list of apstrings called `NameList`. The function must use the two specified functions. Assume that both functions work as specified above no matter what you have written before. In addition, the function should decrement the number of names (numNames) and return a Boolean true if the deletion process was successful (the item was found and deleted) or false if the process was not successful (the item was not found). Write the function `DeleteItem` below with the following conditions:

```
// precondition: apvector NameList holds a specified (numNames) number of ap-
string names
// postcondition: if the DeleteName is found in the NameList, it is deleted,
the numNames value is //decremented by one, and the function returns true;
otherwise the function returns a false.
```

_____

_____

_____

_____

_____

_____

_____

_____

_____

_____

_____

_____

_____

_____

_____

_____

_____

_____

_____

_____

Use the following program to answer questions 10 and 11.

```cpp
// This program displays a trace of the factorial function.

#include <iostream.h>
#include <iomanip.h>

const char INDENT = ' ';
int width;
int factorial(int n);

int main()
{
 int number, result;

 cout << "Enter a number (-1 to quit): ";
 cin >> number;
 while(number != -1)
 {
  width = 0;
  result = factorial(number);
```

```
      cout << "Enter a number (-1 to quit): ";
      cin >> number;
   }

   return 0;
}

int factorial(int n)
{
 int result = 1;
 width++;
 if(n==1)
 {
   cout << setw(width) << INDENT
        << "Entering factorial with n = " << n << endl;
   cout << setw(width) << INDENT
        << "Exiting factorial with result = " << result << endl;
   width --;
   return 1;
 }
 else
 {
   cout << setw(width) << INDENT << "Entering factorial with N = "
        << n << endl;
   result = n*factorial(n - 1);
   cout << setw(width) << INDENT
        << "Exiting factorial with result = " << result << endl;
   width--;
   return result;
 }
}
```

10. Compile and run the factorial program. Test the function with the inputs 1, 2, and 9. Be sure that you understand the behavior of the function.

_____

_____

_____

_____

_____

_____

_____

_____

_____

_____

_____

_____

_____

_____

_____

_____

_____

_____

_____

_____

_____

_____

_____

_____

_____

_____

_____

11. Try running factorial with an input of 0. Explain the behavior of your computer. How could this behavior be prevented?

_____

_____

_____

Use the following code for the program sort.cpp to answer questions 12 – 16.

```cpp
// Program file: sort.cpp
// This program supports the testing of the binary
// search and quick sort algorithms

#include <iostream.h>
#include <ctype.h>
#include <iomanip.h>
#include "apvector.h"

const int MAX_SIZE = 8;
const int LENGTH = MAX_SIZE - 1;
```

```cpp
typedef int element;
typedef int list_type[MAX_SIZE];

int binsearch(element target, apvector<int> &list, int first, int last);
void quick_sort (apvector<int> &list, int left, int right);
void print_list (apvector<int> &list, int first, int last);
void get_list (apvector<int> &list;
void swap(element &x, element &y);

int main()
{
 apvector<int> &list (MAX_SIZE)
 char query;
 int target, position;

 do
 {
  get_list(list);
  print_list(list, 0, LENGTH);
  quick_sort(list, 0, LENGTH);
  print_list(list, 0, LENGTH);
  cout << "Enter target value for search: ";
  cin >> target;
  position = binsearch(target, list, 0, LENGTH);
  if(position > -1)
   cout << "Target is at position " << position << endl;
  else
   cout << "Target is not in list." << endl;
  cout << "Continue? [Y/N]: ";
  cin >> query;
 }while((toupper(query) == 'Y'));
 return 0;
}

void print_list(apvector<int> &list, int first, int last)
{
 cout << "First = " << first << " Last = " << last << endl;
 for (int i = first; i <= last; ++i)
  cout << i << " " << list[i] << endl;
}

void get_list(apvector<int> &list)
{
 for (int i = 0; i < MAX_SIZE; ++i)
 {
  cout << "Enter a number: ";
  cin >> list[i];
 }
```

```
    }

    int binsearch(element target, apvector<int> &list, int first, int last)
    {
     int midpoint;

     if (first > last)
      return -1;
     else
     {
      midpoint = (first + last) / 2;
      if (list[midpoint] == target)
       return midpoint;
      else if (list[midpoint] > target)
       return binsearch(target, list, first, midpoint - 1);
      else
       return binsearch(target, list, midpoint + 1, last);
     }
    }

    void quick_sort (apvector<int> &list, int left, int right)
    {
     int pivot, left_arrow, right_arrow;

     left_arrow = left;
     right_arrow = right;
     pivot = list[(left + right) / 2];      // Determine pivot value.
     do                                     // Move data left or right.
     {
      while (list[right_arrow] > pivot)
       --right_arrow;
      while (list[left_arrow] < pivot)
       ++left_arrow;
      if (left_arrow <= right_arrow)
      {
       swap(list[left_arrow], list[right_arrow]);
       ++left_arrow;
       --right_arrow;
      }
     } while (right_arrow >= left_arrow);
     if (left < right_arrow)                        // Sort left of pivot.
      quick_sort(list, left, right_arrow);
     if (left_arrow < right)                        // Sort right of pivot.
      quick_sort(list, left_arrow, right);
    }

    void swap(element &x, element &y)
    {
```

```
element temp = x;

x = y;
y = temp;
}
```

12. Compile and test the program. Run the program with randomly ordered data values, such as 3, 7, 2, 9, 1, 5, 15, 8. Search for a value in the list and for a value not in the list. Then run the program with data values in strictly ascending order (1,2,3,4,...) and in strictly descending order (...4,3,2,1). Be sure you understand the behavior of the sorting and searching algorithms.

_____

_____

_____

_____

_____

13. Sequential search is a linear algorithm, in that in the average case, it takes $N/2$ comparisons to locate a given target value in a list and in the worst case, it takes N comparisons, for a list of length N. Study the binary search algrorithm in the code above and estimate how many equality comparisons it would take to locate a target value in the worst case, for a list of length N. Try to come up with a formula for the number of comparisons in terms of N.

_____

_____

_____

_____

_____

_____

_____

_____

_____

_____

_____

_____

_____

_____

_____

_____

_____

_____

14. Run the program with test data that demonstrate the worst-case behavior of the binary search function. You may wish to use a counter variable in the function to display the number of comparisons used on each run. How do your results compare with your estimate from the last question?

_____

_____

_____

_____

_____

15. Selection sort is a quadratic algorithm, in that in the average case, the number of comparisons needed to sort a list is roughly N^2, for a list of length N. Study the quick sort algorithm and estimate, first, how many comparisons would be needed to rearrange the data on each recursive call and, second, how many recursive calls would be needed. The product of these two values, in terms of N, represents the amount of work done by the quick sort.

_____

_____

_____

_____

_____

_____

_____

_____

_____

_____

_____

_____

_____

_____

16. Place counters in the quick sort function that maintain the number of comparisons and the number of recursive calls of the function. Run the function with three different data sets, and compare the averages of the counts with your estimates from the last question. How do your results compare? What would the arrangement of the data in the list be like to cause quick sort to have worst-case and best-case behavior?

IN THE LAB

PROJECT 11-1

Write and test a recursive function power that raises a number to the nth power, for n>= 0. The function should take two parameters, the base and the exponent. On each recursive call, the exponent should be decremented by 1. When each recursive call returns, the result should be multiplied by the base and returned. When n = 0, the function should return 1. Compare the results of several runs of this function with the results of running the math library function pow to verify that your function works correctly.

PROJECT 11-2

Write a program that uses a recursive function to sum up all the consecutive odd integers less than a specified odd integer. For example, if the integer specified is 15, the program should calculate 13 + 11 + 9 + 7 + 5 + 3 + 1 = 49.

Test the user's input to make sure s/he has entered an odd number using a statement such as:

```
if(n%2 != 0) // if the remainder after dividing by 2 is not 0, then the number
is odd
```